Green Line 1930 - 1980

Contents

Appendices

written by D.W.K. Jones
and B.J. Davis
with invaluable assistance from
L. Akehurst, A. McCall, L. Norris, G. Robbins, K. Robinson, R.S. Turnbull, The P.S.V. Circle, The Omnibus Society, London Transport, and the London Bus Preservation Group.
ISBN 0-905009-02-9

First published 1980

Rare pre-war colour photograph of T211 at Sevenoaks (M. Gaywood; colour separations courtesy Old Motor Magazine)

Foreword

The name Green Line has been synonymous with express coach services in and around London for fifty years. From the first tentative approaches to coach services by the big bus operators of the 1920s and a variety of pioneering services run by independent companies, came a comprehensive network of routes serving all key towns and villages. The rapid developments, acquisitions and take-overs of the early 1930s provide a fascinating story. Subsequent consolidation, wartime setbacks, and post-war developments and the rapid changes of the last decade are equally fascinating.

In this book we have tried to recreate the atmosphere of the early days and to tell each subsequent stage of the story against the background of circumstances prevailing at the time.. Thus, the reader can compare current practices with the standards over fifty years ago. Several appendices give greater detail about some of the aspects of Green Line over the years.

We would like to thank all those who have assisted in the production, especially the dedicated photographers without whose diligence in recording events this book would not have been possible.

Reigate, January 1980.

Design: Nigel Ferrier
Print: Clifford-Thames Printing Company Ltd.

Green Line's ancestry & conception

First of the line: GF525 was in General red and black livery for the London Windsor service. It later became T155. (L.T.E.).

If you had been living in the suburbs or the country around London in 1930, sooner or later as you waited for the bus to work you would probably have spotted something quite new in public transport passing by. Remember that almost every bus in London and London's countryside at that time was red. This one was green; a single-decker in sage green and black, neatly lined-out and with chromium fittings and polished radiator shell. Only the radiator and the bonnet markings gave it away to the initiated; it was the newly-introduced, technically advanced A.E.C. 'Regal' chassis bearing a 'T' fleet number on its bonnet that proved its common origin with the 'General' fleet. But *was* it a bus? It had an air of quiet, under-stated luxury about it. Its route indicators were more helpful. Both sides, front *and* back, proclaimed such useful services as "Welwyn—London—Reigate" or "Harpenden—London—Great Bookham". In bold gilt capitals with a strong underline, the side panels carried the new fleet name —GREEN LINE.

Very soon, the name was to be seen on nearly every main radial route from London, or on coaches congregating at the interchange points in central London—Oxford Circus, Charing Cross, or later—another innovation—at the Poland Street Coach Station just off Oxford Street.

The pioneer routes were lightly patronised at first. Luxury looked like high prices for ordinary people, and in any case, where did you get on the coaches? They always seemed to be travelling at a fair clip! But astute publicity and summer weekends broke down that sort of resistance very quickly. People found they could spend the day at Windsor for 3/6 return— that is only 17½p—from Charing Cross. And the Saturday and Sunday coaches were filled. If at weekends, why not try the Green Line in the week? If you lived at Barnet or Uxbridge, say, your journey to the office would cost you only 1/6 return (7½p) and take just over half-an-hour in comfort and warmth against nearly an hour with changes by other means for only a copper or two less. Add to this friendly, selected crews, a plentiful supply of free time-tables carried on the coach and the surprising information on every scrap of publicity: "Passengers May Hail or Alight from the Coaches Anywhere En Route" and Green Line's success was assured. The men who had backed

Top: This commercial postcard view shows several Green Line coaches on the Embankment in late 1930. Right: T116 and sixteen others carried red and black livery with East Surrey fleetname in Summer 1930 (L. Norris collection). Opposite: A Green Line coach mingles with other 1932 traffic in Piccadilly Circus (L.T.E.).

SAQUI & LAWRENCE
STATE EXPRESS
CIGARETTES
Schweppes
GENERAL
WHISKY
CHELSHAM
CROYDON
GREEN LINE

The Autocar fleetname distinguishes T65 on the London-Tunbridge Wells service, complete with sideboards (C. Klapper).

Queen Line GN4414 and five similar coaches became T352-7 when the Kings' Cross-Baldock service was acquired (G. Robbins collection).

the launching could breathe again. But who were they, and how did it all happen so quickly?

To answer those questions properly, one must go back a long way—to 1906 in fact, when, believe it or not, Vanguard, the foremost operator of motor buses in London at the time, put on an experimental summer service of double-deck Milnes-Daimler buses from London to Brighton. Road surfaces at the time were mostly steam-rolled, untarred, dusty and unpredictable; heavy vehicle design was in its infancy. Solid tyres and cart springs, together with overheating engines and jerky clutch operation, must have made the journey anything but a picnic. In the end, it was the brakes which failed to hold one 'Vanguard' descending Handcross Hill. It ran off the road and there were a number of casualties. This put paid to long-distance operations of this kind for a long time. After the 1914-18 War there was a revival of interest and many firms pioneered lengthy charabanc services to coast towns, using open, canvas-hooded vehicles of Maudslay, Karrier, Thornycroft, Tilling Stevens and A.E.C. marques, many of them being on War surplus chassis, still on solid tyres.

By the mid-twenties, however, evolution had gone far enough in all the factors involved to pave the way for a great movement on to the roads. The roads themselves were being improved out of all recognition; better surfaces, new "arterial" roads, elimination of danger points and so on. Pneumatic tyres were coming into general use for all but the heaviest vehicles, and the combination of soft tyres and smooth surfaces meant that more sophisticated vehicle and body designs could be introduced within reasonable weight limits. Bus design in particular took a great leap forward in the period 1925-30, shedding the heavy vehicle image overnight with the introduction of lightweight, high speed chassis with advanced transmission and braking systems that in most respects were ahead of contemporary private cars. Typical single deck chassis were the Leyland Tiger, the Gilford 1680T and the A.E.C. Regal. It was this last that was adopted as standard by Green Line.

The demand was there to match the vehicles. With improving economic conditions, people were taking more and more to the day out at weekends, whether to the coast as described above, or to the beauty spots closer to London, a trend which was strongly fostered by the London General Omnibus Company. Their long Sunday bus routes penetrating well into their neighbours' territory, as far out as Reigate, Dorking, Guildford and St. Albans, found economic employment for otherwise idle buses. Significant, too, in the longer-term was the urge to move out of then-smoky London and set up home in the green fields—the "Metroland urge". And indeed the Metropolitan Railway provided well for the Bucks. to Baker Street commuter with money in his pocket. But in between the Metropolitan and other outer-suburban railways there were large areas which could only be developed with cheaper housing if road transport, cheap and convenient, could be laid on.

Many coach operators with experience of the coastal or pleasure trade, and former London bus operators, were quick to seize the opportunity. Between 1927 and

The heavy rear corner bumpers seen on T245 crossing Westminster Bridge were soon removed. Note also the extensive route information (L.T.E.).

West London's handsome Daimler CH6 had built in sideboards but was used as a private hire coach by London Transport (Lens of Sutton collection).

1930 a whole range of what were loosely called Express services sprang up, mostly operating a single service from the operator's home town to points in central London such as King's Cross, Aldgate and Charing Cross (Embankment). Names such as Acme, Bucks Express, Hillman's, Premier Line, Red Rover, Skylark and Strawhatter (from Luton, of course) and a dozen more flashed by. The licensing system was in the hands of the local authorities, and there was little or no co-ordination until 1931, when the Road Traffic Act 1930 came into force and imposed the requirement to justify a need before the required Road Service licence would be granted by the newly-instituted Traffic Commissioner.

Some of the independent operators who started by buying cheap chassis on hire purchase found the repayment and maintenance struggle too much; others laid their foundations well and prospered in a highly competitive field. All added something to the fund of experience which was being accumulated by one Arthur Henry Hawkins. In 1911 Arthur Hawkins founded the East Surrey Traction Company, and was its Managing Director. Under his guidance East Surrey had become the predominant bus operator over a wide area of Surrey and Kent, and had its registered office at Bell Street, Reigate (whence its successor, London Country Bus Services, is directed today). In 1921, East Surrey became the operating agent of the London General Omnibus Company over a wide area South of the Thames, and on 12 June 1929 the L.G.O.C. assumed control of East Surrey, together with its subsidiary Autocar Services Ltd., of Tunbridge Wells. Arthur Hawkins continued as Managing Director. North of London, The National Omnibus and Transport Co. was operating on behalf of the L.G.O.C. services comparable to those of East Surrey in the South.

By July 1930, when the tentative express services of L.G.O.C., East Surrey and National were becoming soundly established, responsibility for coach operations was transferred to a new subsidiary of the L.G.O.C. formed to co-ordinate and develop such services—Green Line Coaches Ltd.

East Surrey had not been idle in the tour and coastal business. As early as Easter 1919, Arthur Hawkins placed in service the first of the Company's charabancs, or open motor coaches. A solid-tyred A.E.C. "Y" type, it was used for day excursions to the sea at Brighton, Worthing or Eastbourne, and to beauty spots in the Home Counties such as Windsor and Hindhead. The range was quickly extended, and six of these 33-seat maroon cars saw extensive service in the early twenties. They had to be supplemented on summer Sundays by K-type double-deck buses on the Brighton run. Six new A.D.C. 419 coaches introduced in 1927 testified to the enduring popularity of these trips. With this experience of coaching behind him, Arthur Hawkins turned his attention to the new market—express coach services to London from Home Counties towns.

First moves were tentative. On 7 August 1928, East Surrey started two trial routes operating every three hours; between Reigate and Northumberland Avenue, London, via Redhill, and between Redhill and Northumberland Avenue via Reigate, thus affording a

London service every hour-and-a-half. Tickets had to be pre-booked. The services were withdrawn on 3 March 1929.

For its own part the L.G.O.C., alarmed by the inroads made by the independents into its traditional weekend country bus operations, had somewhat half-heartedly formed an Express Department in 1928.

Meanwhile, under an initiative of the L.G.O.C. Private Hire Department, a service started on 2 October 1929 between Watford and Golders Green Station forecourt; where passengers could transfer at will to the Underground or to an extensive range of buses into central London. Through bookings to the Underground were offered and a frequent service was run, but these factors alone did not ensure its continuance and it was withdrawn in November. Service was resumed on 18 December 1929, but this time more promisingly on a 30-minute service interval. The timetable quaintly described this as a "General Motorcoach and Underground Rail Service".

Also on 18 December 1929 the L.G.O.C. introduced a 40-minute direct through express service between London (Charing Cross) and Watford. For these routes twenty Reliance all-weather coaches taken from the Private Hire fleet were used and they were housed at the former National garage at Leavesden Road, Watford which the L.G.O.C. re-opened for this purpose. As the L.G.O.C. intended to operate other express coach services a new type of vehicle was needed. The A.E.C. Regal was chosen and T 38, the prototype, was in January 1930 placed in experimental service on the Watford routes. One hundred new coaches were ordered with 27-seat bodies and the first ones appeared initially in a smart livery of "General" red, lined in black and with black above the waistline, and carried a small "General" insignia on the sides. Sufficient of the new T-type coaches were available on 20 April 1930 for the L.G.O.C. to start a Charing Cross—Slough—Windsor service every 30 minutes. Significantly, this route challenged the supremacy of the existing and very popular Premier Line service from Bush House to Windsor which had already been stepped up to a 15-minute interval, and also paralleled for much of its course the L.G.O.C.'s own bus service 81, which took 71 minutes to cover the distance between Hounslow and Windsor, not far short of the time the more comfortable coach would take for the whole journey from London. The coaches were kept at a new garage at Alpha Street, Slough and as new vehicles arrived the service was increased to every 15 minutes, later to 10 minutes.

During May 1930 new T-type coaches in "General"livery replaced the Reliances on the Watford services.

Next, L.G.O.C. sponsored co-operation with the concerns with which it had working arrangements with a view to their starting up express coach services to London. Twelve new T-type coaches were supplied to East Surrey to enable it on 6 June 1930 to commence hourly services to Oxford Circus by separate routes from Redhill, Reigate and Dorking. The coaches carried the red and black livery but with East Surrey fleet name. Five similar T-type coaches were sent to Autocar Services Ltd., so that an hourly service from Tunbridge Wells could start on the same day. Additional new coaches were supplied to both East Surrey and Autocar so that the frequency could be increased to 30 minutes on 24 June.

Such was the situation by the middle of 1930: identical coaches were appearing on radial routes running at regular and frequent service intervals, with common London terminals and identical booking arrangements. The differences, to the public eye, were mainly cosmetic. All that seemed to be lacking was a common identity.

On 9 July 1930 Green Line Coaches Ltd., was registered, with offices at 55 Broadway, SW1. Lord Ashfield, Frank Pick and Daniel Duff were directors of the company as a subsidiary of the London General Omnibus Co. Ltd. Arthur Hawkins was made Managing Director and was given a free hand.

Green Line had arrived.

Right: Red Rover's reserve coach on their London service was this 1930 Dennis EV, which became D2 on acquisition. (E. G. P. Masterman). Opposite: The magnificent interior of T155 with its bobbled curtains, clock and route lettering on the window louvres (L.T.E.).

LONDON GENERAL OMNIBUS CO LD
EMERGENCY DOOR

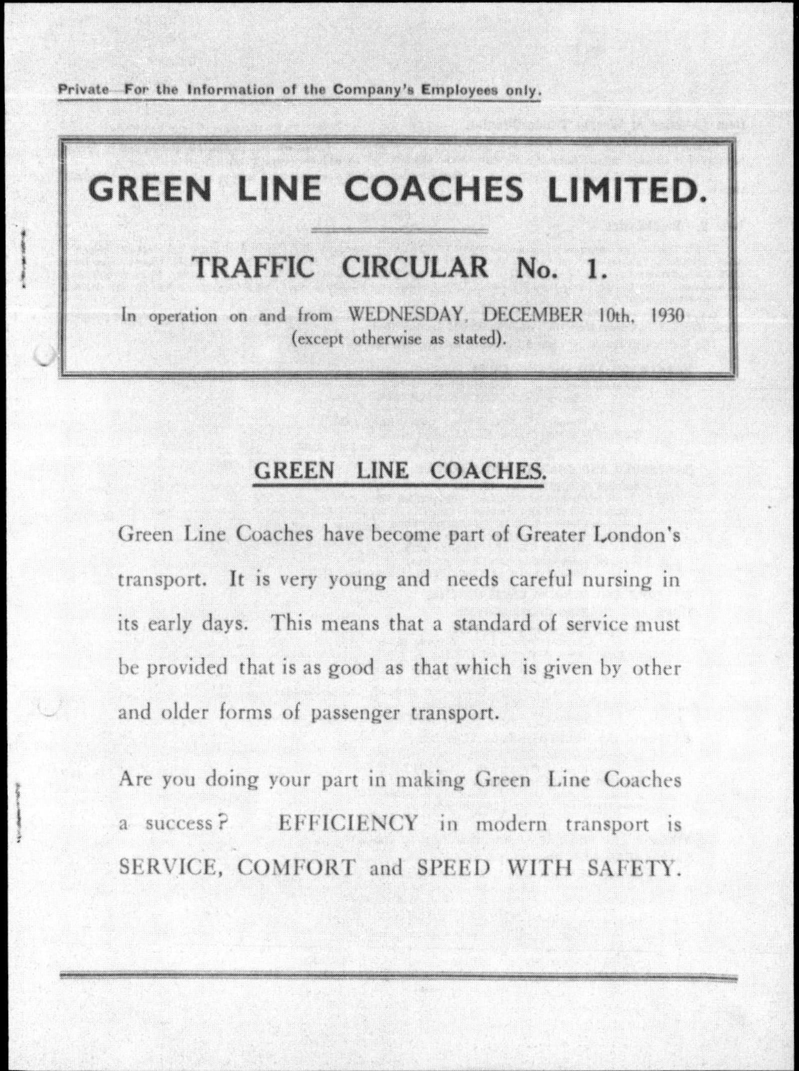

Private For the Information of the Company's Employees only.

GREEN LINE COACHES LIMITED.

TRAFFIC CIRCULAR No. 1.

In operation on and from WEDNESDAY, DECEMBER 10th, 1930
(except otherwise as stated).

GREEN LINE COACHES.

Green Line Coaches have become part of Greater London's transport. It is very young and needs careful nursing in its early days. This means that a standard of service must be provided that is as good as that which is given by other and older forms of passenger transport.

Are you doing your part in making Green Line Coaches a success? EFFICIENCY in modern transport is SERVICE, COMFORT and SPEED WITH SAFETY.

The message of the first Traffic Circular issued by Green Line speaks for itself. These detailed instructions to staff were given to every driver and conductor for nearly 45 years and are a fascinating record of the operations.

Birth and rapid growth

This view of the new Poland Street Coach Station at dusk belies the narrow streets used for access (L.T.E.).

"Green Line Coaches have become part of Greater London's transport. It is very young and needs careful nursing in its early days. This means that a standard of service must be provided that is as good as that which is given by other operators and other forms of passenger transport.

Are you doing your part in making Green Line Coaches a success? EFFICIENCY in modern transport is SERVICE, COMFORT and SPEED WITH SAFETY". (Front page of Traffic Circular No. 1, dated 10 December 1930).

The first coach in the new green livery (T 119) appeared almost immediately after 9 July 1930, and the first route to operate under the Green Line fleetname, Charing Cross to Guildford, started on 17 July—only *eight days* after the birth of the Company; that to Brentwood only a few days later, on 23 July. The first improvised "garage" at London Road, Guildford, was no more than an open yard, with an old 'K' type bus as an office! In other places, too, overnight garaging was improvised hastily, and services were known to start before advance publicity could be distributed. Such was the tempo set by the thrusting team controlling Green Line.

The next eighteen months saw spectacular progress. Some 60 coaches were operated by Green Line and its associates on eight routes in July 1930. By October 1931 there were 275 coaches on 27 routes, and subsequent acquisitions from independent operators took the number over 300 early in 1932.

Green Line did not immediately assume control of operations by its associates which had been started before July 1930. In fact, during the ensuing months a limited amount of development was taking place which to the public appeared to be Green Line, as indeed it was in all essentials, but various reasons such as licensing, ownership of vehicles and staff agreements prevented immediate transfer to Green Line. The L.G.O.C., for instance, inaugurated a Charing Cross—Staines—Windsor service every 30 minutes on 10 July, and followed it with a 60-minute service to Sunningdale on 23 July, later becoming every 30 minutes as vehicles became available. Other routes were opened either by Green Line or its associates as soon as coaches were delivered to run

T225 displays the standard Green Line livery and clear black and white sideboards (J. F. Higham).

Amersham and District's light green and buff livery was worn by T69 until 1933 (D. W. K. Jones).

Ex-Regent Motor Service GF19 (later GF23) outside Poland Street on hire to Skylark in 1932 (J. F. Higham)

The canvas-roofed A.D.C. '419' coaches, like East Surrey PH1207, were used as reliefs in the early '30s (J. F. Higham).

them. In this connection the existence of the L.G.O.C. and East Surrey private hire coaches was invaluable. For example, as deliveries of the new T-type Regals were not sufficient to cover all the new routes in September 1930, East Surrey had to use its own Regal private hire coaches to cover the Oxford Circus—Godstone service. In October, General Reliance all-weather coaches were hired to East Surrey to cover the new Oxford Circus—Chelsham—Oxted route. There was a tendency so far as possible to identify all operations with Green Line: some East Surrey and Autocar coaches while in their former livery would be labelled "This is a Green Line service" and when on 1 October 1930 the L.G.O.C. services to Windsor, Ascot, etc., were formally transferred to Green Line, paper labels were supplied to cover the "General" fleet name with the words "Green Line" and gradually the individual vehicles were painted green. Late in 1930 Green Line inaugurated services from London to Welwyn Garden City, Hertford and Bishops Stortford with the co-operation of the National Omnibus & Transport Co. As an exception to the rule, as late as 26 January 1931 Amersham and District Motor Bus and Haulage Co. Ltd. started a service from Oxford Circus to Amersham using four Green Line Regals in the striking Amersham livery of light green and fawn, with cream wheels. They also displayed a rather finely elaborated fleetname in gilt, from which only the words "and Haulage" were missing. These coaches were T 69, 71, 89, 96 and 104, and they were at that time registered in the name of the Amersham Company.

Detailed enumeration of all the new services and the dates of starting can be found in Appendix f. Some other features of the period of rapid development deserve fuller mention here.

First, publicity. Under Frank Pick's motivation, 55 Broadway had always been highly publicity-conscious. From the start, free leaflets advertising times and facilities were the backbone of Green Line and its predecessors' publicity. In October 1930 was issued the first comprehensive folder under the Green Line label, giving details of all services then running, whether operated by Green Line, East Surrey, General, Autocar or National. This was updated regularly.

The ex-Associated Coaches Leyland Lion, L3 on hire to Skylark at Poland Street (J. F. Higham).

T101 on Route I in June 1934 prior to the extension of the service to Abbots Langley (J. F. Higham).

From 21 February 1931 route letters were introduced on all services to enable the public to identify their coaches more readily—full details appear in Appendix f. Congestion of traffic was rife in London at this time, and criticism centred on the new coach services as one of the causes, particularly because they laid over awaiting their return times in conspicuous places such as Charing Cross (Embankment and Great Scotland Yard) and around Oxford Circus. To avoid this, attention was directed to the creation of long cross-London routes. On 10 December 1930 through workings commenced on Welwyn Garden City—London—Reigate and on Harpenden—London—Great Bookham, followed over the next months by as many other cross-London links as could reasonably be devised.

Another and less successful attempt was made to deal with services which could not readily be linked in this way. On Christmas Day (of all days!) in 1930, Poland Street Coach Station was opened, to give off-street parking and interchange facilities. The trouble was that Poland Street lay in a maze of narrow and congested side streets a few blocks from Oxford Circus, and it was nothing to add ten or fifteen minutes to a journey in the frustrating business of getting into and out of the tangle. The Coach Station itself was a rather hastily-run-up affair with some jazzy green tiling on the facade and precious little manoeuvring room to back it up. Within three years —partly as a result of the findings of a Committee of Inquiry into coach operation in London—it had closed.

A rather happier Christmas present for Green Line was the entry into service, also on 25 December, of the first of a new batch of 100 A.E.C. Regal coaches (T207-306) These were generally similar to the earlier batch (T51-206), but had 30-seat bodies with a forward entrance and sliding door unlike the rear entrance and folding door of the original 27 seaters. The emergency exit was in the rear panels instead of on the offside. The sliding door gave quicker loading than the folding doors at the top of three steps in the first series. One of the second batch—T 219—featured in the Lord Mayor's Show of 1931, and has happily survived to be one of the permanent exhibits in the Museum of London Transport at Covent Garden.

1931 opened with a rush to get new services into operation before 9 February. This was the date set by the Minister of Transport following the passing of the Road Traffic Act 1930 after which no new service should start without a Road Service Licence, and only those services established prior to that date could plead an established facility as a basis for their application to the Traffic Commissioner(s) for a Road Service Licence.

As a consequence, the rest of 1931 did not see such rapid expansion, as much effort had to be expended in obtaining Road Service Licences for existing services, and in planning and justifying to the Traffic Commissioner new proposals and adjustments and extensions designed to give better service to the public. In some of these proposals Green Line were successful, but the heady days of "free for all" were drawing to a close.

Acme's lengthy service to Newmarket operated from the Embankment (E. G. P. Masterman).

T218 displays the new-style two-tone green livery at Windsor Coach Station in October 1935 (J. F. Higham).

By January 1932 it was evident from a number of decisions of the Traffic Commissioner that coaches were being excluded from central London by the expedient of refusing licences. A Committee of Inquiry (The Amulree Committee) was appointed to investigate coach operation in the Metropolitan Area. On 19 April 1932, Frank Pick gave evidence on behalf of Green Line: 50% of passengers on express services wanted to get to the central zone from which it was apparently intended to ban coaches. Green Line traffic was 40% business, 40% shopping, and 20% pleasure. Shopping and pleasure usage was based on convenience. The 40% business element would be forced on to other facilities if coaches were turned short, and more buses would have to be run to take them further in. Mr. Pick advocated a minimum frequency of 30 minutes to retain passenger support, and fixed and advertised stops not more than 1 mile apart.

The Amulree Committee's first Report recommended exclusion from the central area and stopping places at least 2 miles apart, and became the subject of great indignation from coach operators and travelling public alike. Skilful lobbying brought about a Ministerial decision to invite the Committee to review its findings. In the event, the Second Report (August 1932), although still refusing terminal facilities in the Central Area, took a more relaxed tone. Through services were to be allowed to stop at defined points in the Central Area, notably Oxford Circus, Trafalgar Square and Victoria; stopping places at more reasonable distances were to be fixed within the Metropolitan Police Area; and a number of licences which had been previously refused were allowed. Further relaxations were obtained during the ensuing months, but it was not until November 1933 that 134 additional boarding points were authorised following representations to the Metropolitan Traffic Commissioner.

Green Line, recognised that the limits of direct growth had virtually been reached, shifted its energies to the absorption of independent coach operators. By 1932 negotiations were well advanced for the formation of the London Passenger Transport Board, which would have powers of compulsory acquisition of services entering a defined area. In the light of this situation, it is not surprising that by 1 July 1933, when the Board came into being, Green Line had already absorbed a number of its principal competitors. Many were firms of considerable ancestry in the London bus and coach business. Skylark Motor Coach Co. Ltd. was the first to fall (6 February 1932), as it had been one of the first to start, inaugurating a service from Oxford Circus to Guildford as long ago as December 1928. Skylark had also pioneered the through service across London, and by December 1929 was operating Guildford—Oxford Circus—Hertford and High Wycombe—Oxford Circus—Dorking via Reigate. Others followed. The Oxford Circus to Watford service of Bucks Expresses was taken over on 20 February 1932, followed by Regent Motor Services (Oxford Circus to Hertford) on 2 March and Associated Coaches (Ongar) Ltd. (Bishopsgate to Ongar) on 31 March. Later in the year, Blue Belle Motors' hourly service from Paddington to East Grinstead was absorbed (20 July), and on 22 September the old-established Acme Pullman Services was taken over by the L.G.O.C. and forthwith operated as a Green Line service. Acme, alone among these acquisitions, had the distinction of retaining its own fleet name 'ACME' in Green Line publicity and for some considerable time continued to operate far beyond the London area, to Saffron Walden and Newmarket, in fact, until cut back to Bishops Stortford on 1 July 1933 by the boundary definitions of the London Passenger Transport Act 1933. Red Rover Omnibus Ltd. of Aylesbury ceded their limited stop service from that town to Marble Arch on 29 November 1932 and on 26 April 1933 Queen Line Coaches Ltd. handed over their hourly service from King's Cross to Baldock. Finally on 1 July Green Line took over operation of Lewis' Cream Line service to Brookmans Park and West Herts. Motor Services line to Hemel Hempstead. In some instances Green Line took over operation before the formal acquisition of the Company.

Thus in little over a year most of the main competitors on radial coach routes around London had been absorbed. Those that remained would be swept up by compulsory acquisition under the Act of 1933, or, where they ran to points outside the new London Transport area, would survive, subject to certain restrictions on picking-up within the Special area. The "City" service to Southend, Birch Bros' Bedford service, and that run by Farnham Blue Coaches were examples that continued to operate independently.

A good deal of experiment was going on at the same time. Diesel engines had only recently been applied to road transport, but in 1931 three of the latest petrol-engined T-type coaches had been converted to oil fuel. Also a single-deck lightweight A.E.C. bus (The L.G.O.C.'s Q 1), with engine and transmission located on the offside behind the driver's compartment, ran experimentally in coach service in 1932-3, and was the forerunner of 50 specially-constructed Q-type coaches. The biggest problem, then as now, was to handle peak-hour traffic economically, and September 1931 saw the introduction on the heavily-trafficked Bushey—London—Redhill route of LT 1137, a remarkably handsome double-decked six-wheel coach based on one of the Renown chassis used for the L.G.O.C.'s buses. It was not entirely successful in

Top: T255 receives attention in Addlestone Garage, shortly after the garage was opened in 1936 (L.T.E.). Right: The pride of the fleet, double-decker LT1137 picks up at Oxford Circus for Redhill (G. Robbins collection)

Top: Amersham and District garage after acquisition by London Transport (L.T.E.).
Left: This official view of T208 was taken outside the Weymann's works at Addlestone and shows a typical timetable display (L.T.E.).

meeting service requirements, and soon reverted to bus duties.

Green Line's first limited stop service, route BH from Baker Street Station (later Marylebone) to Whipsnade Zoo, was inaugurated on 24 March 1932.

Early in 1932 London General Country Services Ltd, based on the East Surrey headquarters at Reigate was formed as the successor to the East Surrey and National companies, assuming responsibility for peripheral services north and south of the Thames. At the same time (April 1932) the management and administration of Green Line Coaches Ltd. was transferred from 55 Broadway to the Reigate offices of L.G.C.S. Day-to-day operating, traffic and engineering matters had always been closely co-ordinated with the Country Bus side of the business and this change made for greater flexibility of working.

The L.G.O.C. had close working arrangements with the Amersham and District Company to the north west, and area agreements with other neighbouring concerns such as Aldershot & District, and Thames Valley. Thus the area of operations of L.G.C.S. was fairly closely defined when, under the London Passenger Transport Act of 1933, the Company was compulsorily acquired to become part of the London Passenger Transport Board. The acquisition included Arthur Henry Hawkins *and* Green Line Coaches Ltd., with Hawkins taking on the new title of General Manager, Country Buses & Coaches.

The demise of the small operators ended a fascinating era—and a brief look at one gives some insight into a service style which was never to be repeated...

From the start of Green Line services the destination blinds on coaches have been distinctive, normally featuring the fleet name. In 1947 the current amber or yellow colour was adopted making coaches stand out from ordinary buses.

Cream Line's Gilford YY8349 waits for her "regulars" in Northumberland Avenue on a sunny afternoon in 1932 (J. F. Higham).

If Joe Lewis had lived in the seventeenth century he would have been a bold, bad Welsh pirate. As it was he lived in the twentieth century, and in 1930 had a rather run-down, tired-looking garage and private hire business in the High Road at Potters Bar. He also ran a station bus service, for Potters Bar then as now was a dormitory suburb, and the most essential thing about it was to be able to get away from the place. The main link to London—the trains— were steam-hauled, gas-lit, few, dirty and often late.

On 17 September 1930 Green Line Coaches, seeing the opportunity of providing a better service to the locals, opened a new service from Welwyn Garden City via Brookmans Park and Potters Bar to Barnet and Charing Cross.

The point was not lost on Joe Lewis. He decided immediately to run through to London instead of merely serving the station, and before the end of September he had established his route between Brookmans Park and Charing Cross, operating two very smart blue-and-cream Gilford coaches under the name Cream Line. The fares were attractive: 1/3 single and 2/- return from Brookmans Park to London: 1/- and 1/6 from Barnet. Joe was a popular figure in Potters Bar, and by the Spring of 1931 he had four 20-seat Gilfords giving an hourly service for 14 hours a day in direct competition with the Green Line. Even these were unable to cope with the morning and evening peaks and early in 1932 Joe bought a large (second hand) Gilford seating 26 and commonly known to regulars as "All the Nines" from its registration number, GH 9949. Later in 1932 came yet another Gilford, YY 8349, seating 32. And they were packed! How did he do it? For Cream Line was certainly a thorn in the side of the new Green Line service, which of course scrupulously observed timetables, loadings and road safety.

Let's take an early-morning ride to town with Joe Lewis, from New Barnet, say, and find out.

First of all, will he stop? Will he see me? (Remember, no coach stop signs in those days, you just waved mightily). And if the Green Line goes by, that means Joe's already passed. (That was part of the Lewis secret—blow the timetable in rush hours, keep ahead of the Green Line and skim the traffic).

But no, there he is coming under the Station Road railway bridge, just a glimpse and then—out of sight behind a tram. He'll never see me now! Oh, yes, he will—round the *offside* of the tram, a mighty squeal of brakes, and he's stopped a hundred yards up the road. Run for it! And there is Joe himself, as usual on the 8.20, all shirt-sleeves, smiles and cigarette ash: "I was looking out for you, me dear—never miss a regular!" (That was another part of the Lewis secret). Safely away now, and gripping a seat back as you stand, or rather stoop, in the aisle. Fuller than ever, must be nearly forty on board. But Joe slams on the brakes suddenly at Whetstone for three casuals holding up a tentative hand: "Make yourselves at home", he invites them. "Will some of you lie on the floor a bit, please?" And then it's a straight run to the West End, swaying, jolting occasionally as the overtaxed rear springs meet the bumps—but getting there quickly in an atmosphere of cigarette smoke and oil fumes, of chat and good humour—a happy band of pilgrims. And you knew that at 5.20 that evening, you'd find Joe, or one of his drivers, waiting in Northumberland Avenue, the little blue coach usually sitting perkily in front of Green Line's wonderful new double-decker LT 1137, packing them in on the Bushey run. The smile and welcome would be the same as in the morning (and that was the rest of the Lewis secret—loyalty, which his passengers returned).

It couldn't last.

Economics, the Police and legislation were all against the individualist. What the Road Traffic Act of 1930 did not do to limit and regulate fresh activity by the small man, the London Passenger Transport Act of 1933 finished off, setting up a monopoly authority for the London area. The London Passenger Transport Board came into existence on 1 July 1933, and on that day Lewis' Cream Line Coaches did not run. Joe was selling out.

On the following day, the two bigger coaches were to be seen, crewed by uniformed Green Line staff, and running into London only as far as Portman Square. One service had only three passengers. Truncated and impersonal, Route BR, as it became, did not flourish, and on 3 October 1933 it vanished for ever in the course of a re-organisation of Green Line routes.

It is interesting to note that when Green Line Coaches Ltd. was registered on 9 July 1930, three other companies were registered under L.G.O.C. auspices: Red Line Coaches Ltd., Yellow Line Coaches Ltd., and Blue Line Coaches Ltd. with the intention of securing copyright to these names against possible competitors. "Cream Line" was thus an ingenious evasion of this intention on Joe Lewis' part.

Opposite, top left: The 13 seat Saurer from West London Coaches shares Amersham Garage forecourt with two ex-Amersham and District Regals (D. W. K. Jones). Top right: Leyland Tiger KR1168 still carries Maidstone and District livery but was originally a Redcar coach. It became TR39 (D. W. K. Jones). Bottom left: Few passengers used route BR, the temporary home of ex-Lewis Gilford GH9949, and it was soon withdrawn (D. W. K. Jones). Bottom right: Ex Prince Omnibus Company TR35 at Eccleston Bridge in 1937 (D. W. K. Jones).

GREEN LINE

TUN-WELLS, TONBRIDGE, BROMLEY, CATFORD, LEWISHAM, CHARING + VICTORIA.
TUN-WELLS LONDON
GREEN LINE
LONDON TRANSPORT

CREAM LINE

TUMBRIDGE WELLS
GREEN LINE
MY 5029

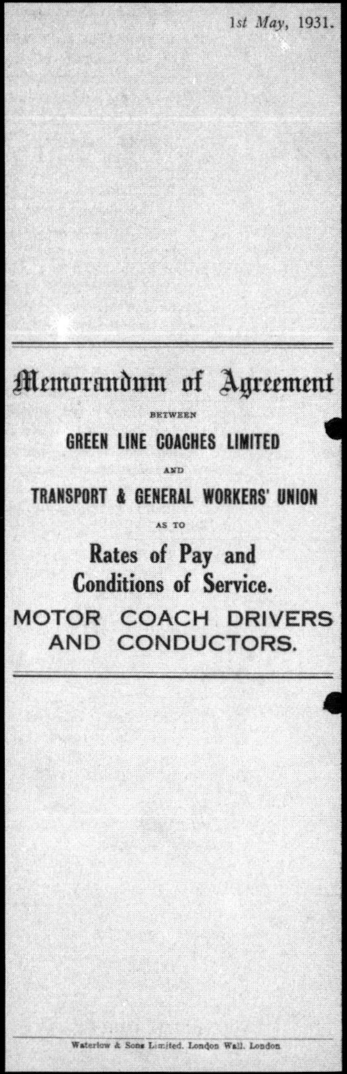
1st May, 1931.

Memorandum of Agreement

BETWEEN

GREEN LINE COACHES LIMITED

AND

TRANSPORT & GENERAL WORKERS' UNION

AS TO

Rates of Pay and
Conditions of Service.

MOTOR COACH DRIVERS
AND CONDUCTORS.

Waterlow & Sons Limited. London Wall. London.

Throughout the history of Green Line detailed agreements with the Transport and General Workers' Union have governed the working practices and conditions of drivers and conductors. The 1931 agreement illustrated is very similar to the current ones, except for the wages – in 1931 a driver earned £3.15s.0d per week for a 48 hours week!

Order out of confusion

GK445 (later TR23) still displays its previous ownership on the indicator at Windsor in 1934. (J. F. Higham).

Almost imperceptibly to the general public, the London Passenger Transport Board began its operating existence on 1 July 1933. The new Board had the monopoly of public road passenger transport within a wide-reaching Special Area around London, and power to operate or to reach agreement over operations in an area generally within 25-30 miles of Central London. Green Line Coaches merged with the Country Bus division, but the fleetname "Green Line" and its distinctive identity have been retained to this day.

Green Line had grown enormously in only three years, and the rapid absorption of a number of independent coach operators was hardly completed by July 1933: now another wave of new routes, new problems, but not alas new vehicles to cope with them, was imminent. For it was a regrettable fact that many of the coaches taken over were light vehicles which had, not surprisingly, been run into the ground in anticipation of the takeover. Other responsible operators such as Premier Line and Queen Line had standards as high as Green Line's own, and their coaches were a valuable asset in a desperate situation.

On 1 July 1933 Green Line and its associates found themselves in control of 446 coaches of 12 distinct makes and many more different types. When all the acquisitions scheduled under the Act of 1933 had been made, the number of coaches that had been dealt with totalled 650 of 15 makes of all sorts, conditions and ages—a daunting proposition. Not all these were in use at any one time, of course. Many underwent complete overhaul amounting to reconstruction, or were repaired for limited further service, while others were condemned outright. Whichever course, the volume of additional work was great. In two years Green Line's rolling stock had grown from a reasonably standardised A.E.C. fleet of under 300 coaches to a very mixed bag over 1] times that size, with all the attendant problems of spares, maintenance and serviceability. Appendix b shows a breakdown of operators and vehicles concerned.

Since one could not produce new vehicles overnight, a start was made on re-organising schedules to eliminate overlapping. Probably the most far-reaching re-organisation of Green Line routes was that which took place on 4 October 1933, following the findings

Top: The original road hog in Epping High Street does not seem to interest the coach conductor. Right: Hillman's No. 124 became GF112, but still carries the smart blue and white livery in this view (D. W. K. Jones).

Top: An ex-Maidstone & District Tiger still carries original livery, but with Green Line fleetname (J. F. Higham).
Left: Ex-Premier Line GC6846 has a Green Line sticker on its claret and cream colours in early 1934 (D. W. K. Jones).

of the Amulree Committee into coach operations in London. As a result, fixed stopping places for coaches were introduced within the Metropolitan Police District, while restrictions placed on the use of many roads in Central London led to the closing of Poland Street Coach Station. Extensive use was therefore made of Eccleston Bridge, Victoria, as a London interchange point, and additional through routes were introduced. All routes were re-lettered, and provision made for 'gaps' to be filled by forthcoming acquisitions. (For details see Appendix f). Thus all Green Line services became Limited Stop, except at the outer ends of some routes.

The second Annual Report of the L.P.T.B. referred to the damaging effect of the Amulree findings on the usefulness of the Green Line services. Receipts and passengers carried were down by a quarter, but mileage had been reduced only by 9%. From being a money-spinner, Green Line had become something of a liability on the rest of the Board's operations, and so remained for a considerable time.

An attempt to secure more economic use of the available vehicles was the introduction on 16 May 1934 of 1d. fares on the outer sections of coach routes—an arrangement which helped to fill many of the empty seats found towards the rural end of some routes, and which enabled parallel bus routes over sparsely-populated stretches to be withdrawn and the buses used to better advantage elsewhere.

The biggest headache lay in keeping on the road all the miscellaneous coaches which could not entirely be dispensed with until new vehicles of standard types were available in sufficient numbers. Fortunately, perhaps, most of the independent operators, led by Edward Hillman's Saloon Coaches, had favoured one make, the Gilford, of which (taking buses and coaches together) nearly 200 were acquired. This was a cheaply-made chassis, available on generous hire-purchase terms, and not designed for a long life; but it had a lion-hearted engine. The decision was made to rehabilitate suitable Gilfords, and to dedicate Reigate Garage to a superhuman effort to sort them out. A few were condemned or sold off; many were turned over to bus work; gradually the best were concentrated at Romford Garage to work the former Hillman high-frequency services into Town, while

L8 in the first Leyland numbering series came from Maidstone and District and later became TR12 (J. F. Higham)

Ex-Queen Line T354 shows the cast metal fleet number introduced in 1932 (J. F. Higham).

others became a valuable "second line" at other garages to cope with peak hours and weekend rushes.

The other large-scale acquisition was of Leyland Titans and Tigers mainly from Premier Line. These were stoutly built vehicles and did grand service up to 1938. They were concentrated mainly at Slough, Bath Road, Windsor and Staines to keep down the variety of spares to be held at garages.

Most of the minor makes disappeared within a year or two, some being condemned without even being repainted in green, while others with more luxurious bodywork were turned over to Private Hire as related in appendix a.

The work put through at Reigate Garage in those early months was incredible. Main garage and workshop for the Country Bus and Coach fleet, it had to cope with overhauls and repairs and demands for spares as usual; most of the available floor-space was littered with dismembered Gilford bodies and chassis of varying descriptions, hues and states of decay—cannibalisation was rife in order to make one presentable vehicle out of two doubtful ones; and all the time the day-to-day comings and goings of a busy bus and coach depot had to be maintained without fail.

Other operators' services acquired during this period included the considerable business of Amalgamated Omnibus Services & Supplies, operating Batten's Coaches between Aldgate, Grays and Tilbury (23 December 1933); Price's Super Coaches between East Ham and Aveley (1 December 1933); West London Coaches' Victoria to Aylesbury service (17 January 1934); and Hill's well-patronised "Strawhatter" service of sleek green Gilford's between King's Cross and Luton (1 February 1934). Others acquired were Sunset Pullman Coaches and Fleet's all-night service on the Romford road, the coaches operated by Sunshine Saloons of Kingston and the Prince Omnibus Co. Among these acquisitions of independent coach operators totalling close on thirty, perhaps two stand out by reason of their size and dynamic enterprise—Premier Line Ltd. and Edward Hillman's Saloon Coaches Ltd.

Hillman opened a limited stop service between Stratford and Brentwood in December 1928; this was the pioneer express service in the London area where tickets were issued on the coach and a short headway maintained. The service was first extended to Chelmsford and then Colchester, and in 1930 to the Essex coast. By the beginning of 1931, such was the popularity of the service that 57 Gilford coaches were maintaining Hillman's services from Bow Road to points in East Anglia as far afield as Norwich and Yarmouth. Frequent services continued to be offered on the inner sections of the route, Bow to Romford and Brentwood. With an associate company, Upminster Services Ltd., the total Hillman fleet was 92, all Gilfords with the exception of a fine 6-wheeled A.E.C. Renown coach. Hillman had turned his attention also to building up air services from an airfield at Romford before he died on the last day of 1934 at the early age of 45.

Hillman's 123 became GF111 (L. Norris collection).

T162 on Route I at Crawley (M Gaywood).

Ex-Red Rover Dennis Arrow at Radlett (D. W. K. Jones).

Sunset Pullman Gilford EV6877 (E. G. P. Masterman).

On 10 January 1934, London Transport assumed responsibility for the Hillman and Upminster workings in the London area, Green Line being the operating agent, with 65 coaches and a staff of 300. From then on, the distinctive blue-and-white Hillman coaches carried a red label with the Board's address, and until repainted often had a "Green Line" fleetname added on the side panels. 22 more coaches were transferred on 13 August 1934, including the 6-wheeled "Renown", following transfer of the longer-distance journeys to Eastern National.

It says much for the aggressive development of both the Hillman and Green Line services in this sector that the most intensive coach service in London (and probably anywhere else too) became that between Aldgate and Ilford. Green Line and former Hillman and Sunshine Pullman workings combined to provide a 5-minute headway to Brentwood; the former Upminster Services similarly worked on a 5-minute headway between Aldgate and Upminster, and there were also some night workings. To give an example, an early 1934 timetable shows that service commenced with the 3.17 a.m. coach from Romford to Upminster and ended with the arrival of the 1.55 a.m. from Upminster working into Romford Garage nearly 23 hours later!

Equal in size and pioneering spirit was the Premier Line organisation, but different in its history largely because of licensing difficulties which led to great efforts to devise new routes and get them into operation.

The name "Premier" had associations with London bus operations over many years. By the late twenties Premier Omnibus Co. Ltd. was running a well-kept fleet of buses in London, mainly Leyland Titans in distinctive chocolate and cream livery. With this solid base of experience Premier launched into the short-distance express business with a London—Windsor coach service starting on 27 January 1930. When the initial order for 19 Leyland Titan coaches was complete, Premier were able to offer a 15-minute headway with a through fare of 3/6 return and season ticket facilities. Subsequently, in 1930 Premier Line Ltd. was formed as the coaching subsidiary of Premier. Routes were planned to London from Farnham Common, Guildford, Aylesbury and

Top: R37 was an ex-Batten's Reliance allocated to Addlestone for route C1. In this 1937 view it stands outside the private hire garage at Brixton (D. W. K. Jones). Right: GF166 came from Beaumonts and here waits to start duty at Romford (D. W. K. Jones).

Top: Ex-Strawhatter Gilford GF100 on service X in 1936 (D. W. K. Jones). Left: T355 came from Queen Line and originally looked like its sister T354 (see p.26). It acquired a Weymann all-metal body in 1935 (Lens of Sutton collection).

Sunbury Common, and from Windsor to Maidenhead and to Aylesbury, and orders were placed for a large number of Leyland Tiger coaches to operate them. Not all the coaches were delivered in time to get the routes started before 9 February 1931, that is, in time to beat the licensing restrictions to be imposed on new routes from that day under the terms of the Road Traffic Act 1930. Ultimately, after many vicissitudes, all but the Guildford service ran in some form or other; but whereas before 9 February Premier Line appeared to have too few vehicles, now it had too many to operate the services for which it had been able to obtain licences.

Attention turned to finding an outlet for the surplus vehicles in the expansion of bus business radiating from Aylesbury, under the fleet name "Aylesbury Line". The Act of 1933 made provision for splitting the Premier enterprises between London Transport and (so far as the Aylesbury undertaking was concerned) operators in adjoining areas, such as Eastern National, United Counties, Thames Valley and City of Oxford. 18 of the Leyland Tiger coaches and all 19 of the Titan coaches were transferred to London, and all eventually found employment on Green Line services. Largely they remained for a while on their old routes, where their claret-and-cream livery was initially altered by the substitution of "Green Line" transfers on the side panels. Later, along with other Leyland buses and coaches, they were grouped at certain garages in the west, mainly at the former Premier Line premises at Bath Road, Slough and later at Staines and Windsor.

A third allocation of route letters was made with effect from 5 June 1935. The main innovation was that the subsidiary workings previously using a prefix 'A' or 'B' now took a numeral suffix, i.e. AH becoming H2 and so on, although the route BH did not become H3 until 20 July 1936.

It was several years before the style of fleet-name used on publicity material became settled. Many alterations were tried, until the familiar bulls-eye used until 1969 was established.

A line-up of new 10T10 coaches being prepared for service in 1938 (L.T.E.).

The first of the long-awaited new generation of vehicles arrived towards the end of 1936. These were fifty front-entrance 30-seat A.E.C. Regals of 9T9 type. They were quickly followed by the fifty 32-seat A.E.C. 6Q6 type with side-mounted engine, developed from the original Q 1.

1937 brought the testing on service of an advanced new vehicle, TF 1, designed and built by Leyland Motors Ltd. in consultation with the engineers of London Transport, specifically for London coach service. The engine lay on its side beneath the floor. 87 more underfloor-engined coaches of TF type came into service in 1939, twelve of them being provided with special bodies which included observation windows in the roof for use on private hire and tours in Central London.

Meanwhile, a further development on more conventional lines, the 10T10 type A.E.C. Regal was ordered in large numbers, and was to form the mainstay of the fleet for many years. 266 in all were delivered in 1938 and 1939. These new types offered great advances in passenger safety and comfort. Technical details of all the types mentioned above are dealt with in appendix d, and we are fortunate that one of each type is preserved as a lasting memorial to the sound engineering design of the era.

With the coming of the 9T9 and the 6Q6 vehicles, the Gilfords were rarely if ever seen on Green Line duty, doubtless to the great relief of maintenance and operating staff alike. Similarly, but with infinitely greater regret, the advent of the 10T10s enabled the Leyland Tigers and Titans to go into honourable retirement. Maintenance of the bodywork of the original "Regals", especially those of the T207-T306 series, had become an expensive problem, and the 10T10s would have made it possible to take some off the road for bracketing and other extensive repair, had not the process been halted by the outbreak of war.

As the rolling stock replacement programme gathered way, it once again became possible to resume orderly development of the services offered to the public. A Green Line Guide in booklet style had been available in 1933, after which coach times were included in the monthly area bus timetables from July 1934. In 1936

Top: T475 passes Grosvenor Gardens, Victoria with a "via Croydon Airport" slipboad (L. Norris collection). Right: Another 10T10 showing the orange, black and white slipboards with alternative terminals (L. Norris collection). Opposite: T647 waits between duties at Aldgate (H. F. Adcock).

GREEN LINE Z1
GRAYS
LONDON
STEPNEY
POPLAR
WEST HAM
EAST HAM
BARKING
DAGENHAM
RAINHAM
WEST THURROCK
GRAYS
2
EYK 277
Not "Brown" Bread

Coaches lay-over at Aldgate just before the war (L. Norris collection).

Interior of Q type shows the long seat over the engine.

 Conductor and mechanical arms signal as Q205 circles Marble Arch (L.T.E.)

Top: The unusual engine position of the TF required side access (L.T.E.). Left: Rare view of 9T9 in coach service before the war (L. Norris collection).

there came the first comprehensive Green Line Coach Guide. It contained times, fares, weekly and four-weekly season rates, boarding points, maps and diagrams and a list of Country Area bus routes, all for 2d. Subsequent issues were even more ambitious, with a good deal of matter in chatty style about objects of interest near the routes, shopping centres, museums, nature notes and (inevitably) 32 pages of local advertising in a specially-tinted section, still selling for 2d! More matter-of-fact were later issues, quick and easy reference coming to be regarded as more to the point than rural ramblings. Strangely, it was not until 1937 that green was adopted as the prevailing colour for the vast output of timetables, guides and route maps, much early publicity being in navy blue or black.

Much research was being done to improve schedules and services to cater for the changing and ever-growing public needs. Though only two entirely new routes were introduced between 1936 and 1939, there were constant revisions, diversions and extensions of existing services to improve the cover given. There was also a pattern of seasonal alteration to meet the summer peak traffic, particularly at the weekends when every resource in men and machines had to be turned out to cope with the crowds. But more on that subject later.

These were perhaps the golden years of Green Line development, when the rewards of foresight, careful planning and aggressive commercial selling policies began to roll in. If one had to name one factor on which the popularity of Green Line Coaches was especially based, it would be the availability of cheap return tickets and even cheaper season tickets. Once the Green Line habit was established it held good for weekend trips and working days alike.

Then the War struck Green Line like a bomb. All services were halted even before war was declared. How the disrupted organisation was painfully put together again under wartime conditions, only to be struck down a second time, and how Green Line was rebuilt after the War is told in later chapters. Before that, let us see how pre-war Green Line looked from the passenger's viewpoint.

Green Line quickly realised the value of its services to the countryside lover and published many books and pamphlets giving descriptions of attractive walks with detailed travel instructions. London Transport continues to publish its series of Country Walks books.

Riding the Green Line in the Thirties

T223 awaits departure from Oxford Circus in 1934. The 'E' prefix to the fleetnumber indicates allocation to a former East Surrey service (L.T.E.)

LONDON TRANSPORT
LONDON TRANSPORT
AK
LONDON - BALDOCK
AK
LONDON - BALDOCK
GREEN LINE

Opposite: Stevenage High Street in August 1934 with ex-Queen Line T354 just before its withdrawal for rebodying as a bus (L.T.E.). This page: T232 was rebodied with a very smart M.C.W. all-metal body in 1933 and is seen (top) before entering service and (left) in 1937 having acquired ordinary sideboards in place of the inset displays over the windows. (L.T.E. and L. Norris collection).

You raise your hand. The big green coach glides obediently to a halt. The door opens and you are gathered in—you, your parcels and bags, all gathered from the cold and wet into the warmth and quiet of your own 'magic carpet'. A welcoming smile from the conductor and a protective arm as he guides you to your seat and places your baggage in the rack above you. Enter the world of Green Line, 'thirties-style.

Settle down and look around you. It's hard to define the special atmosphere that pervaded Green Line in those days—something between a taxi and first-class air travel (as it was then). An air of modest luxury, perhaps? Your deep-sprung seat absorbs most of the road shocks. The seats are upholstered in a neutral, fine-quality beige cord. Nothing flamboyant either in the harmonising decor— discreet curtains, few visible notices, no advertisements—just a subtle touch of green here and there, and the legend "Green Line Coaches Ltd." on the front panel to remind you in whose care you are. Only the clock on the front bulkhead and the heater below it sparkle with chromium. Otherwise, all is subdued and above all, quiet. Suddenly, you have it—it is the sense of being *insulated* from the traffic, from the worries and discomforts of other travel, from day-to-day cares, that used to make your journey by Green Line part of the pleasure of your holiday or your shopping trip, not just a regrettable necessity.

Then, soon after boarding, came the infinitely soothing Ticket Ceremony. After asking to know your destination (and remember, it might easily be an obscure turning out of the main road, with not a house in sight, some 40 miles away on the other side of London), the Conductor would consult the Book of the Words, which lived in a large metal box. Once the Oracle had told him the correct fare, he would withdraw an enormous Ticket Rack from the same box, and ultimately, after various incantations and operations with Bell Punch and nippers, money would change hands and a ticket would be given into your keeping. But such a ticket! Of length hitherto unknown and selected from a wide range of attractive colours! There must be many a grown man around still who, as a boy, longed to board the coach, at, say, Hitchin, and ask for a Half Return to Reigate in the hope that something really exotic would be fished out of the depths of the box to cover such a rare trip.

Not a little of the credit for the feeling of security must go to the coach crews. Mostly hand-picked for the job, their courtesy and consideration for the passenger were outstanding. Their smart green uniform, topped in summer with a gleaming white cap cover, and their impeccable timekeeping contributed to the confidence that must have imparted itself to the frailest of little old ladies emboldened to sample the new form of transport. At principal stopping-places and of course at interchange points there were regulators at hand to help and advise and iron out traffic problems, not the least of their duties being to marshal weekend queues in an orderly fashion and to call up whatever reserves could be made available to meet anticipated return loadings.

This was another aspect of Green Line service. A fine Sunday morning could bring out untold numbers of people, all anxious to get out into the country quickly. Queues up to a quarter-mile long have been known at Eccleston Bridge, Victoria. To a degree, experience helped in forecasting likely demand and providing relief coaches within limits of availability. But the return in the evening was another matter. If the day stayed fine, people would put off coming back until dark; then it was like a tidal wave. Whereas outward journeys had been spread, everybody wanted to return about the same time.

From Amersham and Aylesbury, Westerham and Windsor and Wrotham and Watford and Whipsnade they flowed. Whipsnade Zoo—that was a star attraction which had only just opened. In March 1932 Green Line started its first Limited Stop service, from Marylebone Station to Whipsnade, picking up only at Golders Green and Barnet. A sparse weekday service became half-hourly on Sundays and Bank Holidays in summer, and it was an instant success. It was not unusual to see the service coach followed closely by five or six more, pressed into service from all parts and all bulging with people. There would be elderly Daimler '419' types, A.E.C. Reliance private hire coaches, both with canvas roofs, and Gilford coaches from as far afield as Romford. On the other side of the Thames at hop-picking seasons thousands would leave London for Kent for a family reunion with the pickers each weekend. At times like these even the occasional double-decker bus would be brought up—a real queue-clearer that, and answer to the prayer of hard-pressed regulating staff. Anything that would travel was brought in, regardless of expense, to keep the crowds cheerful and get them home, well, at least before midnight. As one elderly driver reminisced: "No need to hang about, mate, you'd got a full load, so you just put your foot down and b.... went".

The public did not see the half of it, though. Behind the scenes, marvels of improvisation were performed each weekend by operational and office staff alike, all aiming to see that there were enough seats in the right place at the right time. In the nature of things, they could not succeed every time; but whatever could be achieved was done by up-to-the-minute information by telephone, by persuasion of crews to turn round and do that bit more, by sheer devotion, and, at bank holidays and summer weekends by borrowing up to 200 red double deck buses.

Other ways of easing the heavy return movement into London were in force during the years when return tickets were issued universally. In 1931 return tickets issued in London were made valid for return to London by any other Green Line route; and from 1935 passengers holding return tickets for journeys back to London were allowed to travel by rail after 4.00 p.m. on Saturdays and Sundays. This facility proved quite popular.

The weekend rush was to some degree repeated in the years following the War, when even if people had cars, they hadn't the petrol to run them any great distance, and the crowds flooded back to public transport for their day out.

Right: Rural scene with elaborate L.T. shelter and ex Red Rover Dennis at Chalfont St. Giles (L.T.E.). Opposite: Atmospheric interior view of an ex-Maidstone & District Leyland Tiger Coach (L.T.E.).

GREEN LINE COACHES
RETURN TICKETS
LOST PROPERTY
FIRST AID

London Transport is to engage women conductors for green country buses and Green Line coaches. Women between 23 and 35 are invited to apply at the L.P.T.B.'s country garages. Here's the uniform. Pay is £2 14s. a week plus war wage rising to £3 4s. plus war wage.

War brought about many dramatic changes, some of which were to become normal in the years that followed. The arrival of women conductors received a considerable amount of publicity which was repeated thirty years later with the advent of women drivers – the latter are now more common than the former!

Wartime Green Line: Services Y, Z1 and Z2 reopened on 1 November 1939, the day these two STLs were recorded at Aldgate (D. W. K. Jones).

Without warning all Green Line coaches were withdrawn from service on the evening of 31 August 1939, although some may have run from Romford for a day or two longer. Within hours on the following day nearly 400 of them had been converted into ambulances fully equipped to take eight or ten stretcher cases, and most were transferred immediately from their country garages to the London area, where they came under the orders of the Ministry of Health. This astonishing feat had been rehearsed and sample conversions carried out at the time of the Munich crisis in 1938. This time it was the real thing, and the coaches were standing by, in or close to London Transport garages where they could be manned quickly in the event of large-scale emergency, well before war was declared on 3 September.

Green Line services had ceased to exist, apart from a few replacing buses on outer sections of routes previously covered by coaches only, and some sporadic north-eastern area operation by red buses. By 25 September eleven such bus services were operating, and on 1 November express services re-started with green double-deckers operating at Green Line fares from Aldgate to Romford (Y1 every few minutes—half-hourly to Brentwood) and Grays: Z1 and Z2 every 15 minutes). Gradually, however, sufficient coaches were released to start up a number of services. By 8 May 1940, fourteen of the more important routes were operating again, and continued until the Autumn, when the start of the blitz on London resulted in cross-London services being withdrawn and all routes terminated in Central London. To regularise this arrangement, and to replan the network to suit wartime needs, routes were reorganised on 4 December 1940, and additional routes reinstated then and on 18 December. 33 routes were then in operation, numbered between 2 and 59 (some with suffix letters) in place of the letters used since 1931. The numbers were selected so as not to clash with those of Central bus services running over common sections of route. Details are to be found in Appendix f.

To provide sufficient rolling stock for the additional facilities, many of the early petrol-engined T-type coaches were recalled from store.

The "numbered" routes terminated at Aldgate,

Green Line ambulances: T499 at Henden (top), Q226 at St Thomas' Hospital with Emergency Medical Services "EMS" triangle (right) and TF69 and TF23 at Chalk Farm (opposite) (all D. W. K. Jones).

AMBULANCE
EMS
FJJ 766
GREEN LINE
AMBULANCE
FJJ 634

Reinstated T714 looks very smart in the Summer of 1940 (D. W. K. Jones).

An STL covers the Sevenoaks – Tunbridge Wells section of C1 (J. F. Parke)

Oxford Circus or Victoria, and did not run late in the evening: it must be remembered that apart from bombing hazards in Central London, drivers faced long miles of impenetrable darkness in the countryside, with only a glimmer of light from a masked headlamp to help.

Conditions inside were claustrophobic, too, with no light worth speaking of, certainly not to read by, and netting pasted over the windows, except for a small diamond shaped aperture through which one could see—nothing.

It was no mean achievement to have set up a fresh network of fairly close-headway routes under wartime conditions, taking into account the loss of experienced staff, the increasing difficulties of maintenance and the disruption caused by bombing all through the winter of 1940-41. The burden on the Country Area as a whole was immense at this time; dispersal of families from inner London was at its peak; factories concerned in the war effort were more and more located out of the vulnerable central area, and the result expressed in terms of journeys to work either locally or to London was a heavy extra strain on an organisation suffering like everyone else from shortage of staff and stock. For Green Line, the difficulty was overcome for the time being by the introduction on heavy-traffic routes of double-deck vehicles. For this purpose some 180 STL-type buses were transferred from the Central Buses fleet and repainted in green livery.

The special war-time coach system was not to remain undisturbed for long. As shortages of fuel and rubber became more pressing, it was decided that all Green Line services would again be withdrawn, the last day of operation being 29 September 1942. Thus the struggle for survival was lost, and the name "Green Line" vanished for 3½ years.

Most of the 10T10 coaches were taken over for military purposes, a large number being employed by the U.S. Forces as ambulances and mobile canteens ("Clubmobiles"). After D-day, early 7T7 type were shipped to the Continent to help in the movement of displaced persons, and eventually these were dispersed far and wide. Records exist of T355 and T392 being seen at Hanover Transit Camp in 1946; of a 6Q6 working a local service in Algeciras, Spain, and of three separate operators in the Douai district of France using 7T7s liberated from military use well into 1948. No doubt there were many similar instances elsewhere. Some, such as T55, stayed in this country and were used by War Agricultural Executives to ferry Italian prisoners of war working on the land to and from their billets.

One might wonder what happened to the Green Line regular passengers who found themselves so abruptly without transport in 1942. In April 1944, London Transport investigated just that. The somewhat dubious conclusions reached were: 50% not travelling; 20% on Country buses; 10% on Central Buses; under 10% by rail; a negligible amount on trams, trolleybuses and Underground. That adds up to 90%. The other 10% is unexplained—call-up and evacuation may have had something to do with it.

Above: the numbering of routes is illustrated by T711 and an STL (L. Norris collection) Right upper: An STL on Route 58 on a bleak winter's day in 1941 (J. Dodkins). Below: USA 201123 disguises T648 as an American Red Cross transport vehicle (L. Norris collection). Right lower: A number of early T's found their way onto the farm during the war (D. W. K. Jones).

Stopping places had to be defined by stop signs as a result of 1930's regulation and a variety of stop designs has been used over the years. Outside the GLC area the old London Transport designs are now being replaced by the Department of Transport standard design.

Post-war recovery

T695 illustrates the post-war way of things – amber blinds, green and gold sideboards and two-tone livery. The scene is Sevenoaks Bus Station (Lens of Sutton).

The war years had brought a social transformation in the country areas around London. Many of the vast numbers who moved out of Inner London during the war preferred to stay on in the countryside or the towns of the Home Counties. New work places had sprung up all over the area; new shopping and leisure habits, and a new pattern of living emerged which was for most people a better way of life. The resultant demands for transport had been met in war time as well as could be in the circumstances; in fact the wartime traffic carried by Country Bus and Green Line together rose to as much as double that of pre-war days. Once the war was over, the tight restrictions on supply of new private cars, petrol rationing, and the fact that everyone was on the move after the rigid pattern of wartime living, added up to a well-nigh insatiable demand for public transport.

With the end of the War in Europe in 1945, thoughts turned to the re-introduction of the Green Line system. Vehicles began to return from the U.S. Forces and other war duties and an immense task faced London Transport's engineers in rehabilitating the coaches for normal passenger service. Some were little better than battered neglected shells.

A heavy strain also fell on headquarters and local staff in arranging routes and training sufficient staff to man the vehicles under conditions where claims on resources throughout the organisation grew faster than the supplies to meet them. Nevertheless, the first two post-war Green Line services commenced on 6 February 1946 (715 Hertford-London-Guildford and 720 Bishops Stortford to Aldgate, both at 30 minute intervals). With the introduction of these routes a new numbering system was employed, the now familiar '700' series, as still in use today.

During the first half of 1946 steady progress was made with the introduction of routes, until a complete system of 26 routes was in operation by mid-July. For the first time, however, the return tickets which had been a familiar feature of Green Line since its inauguration were missing. A limited series of cheap day return tickets was introduced from 1 October 1946 to and from London and lasted with various modifications until the fares revision of October 1950, after which returns virtually disappeared for many years.

Top, left to right: The busy post-war years needed many relief coaches – coach Q213 and bus Q80 at Victoria in June 1949 (both A. B. Cross), T561 passes through a busy Dartford Market Place on 701 (Lens of Sutton). Bottom, left to right: Another relief, this time 9T9 T433 at Kingston (A. B. Cross), Tilbury is the destination of TF73 at Aldgate (J. F. Higham), a popular 720 journey worked by TF31 (A. B. Cross).

Essolube
SWAN VESTAS
GREEN LINE RELIEF
712
LUTON
LONDON TRANSPORT
CGJ 185

ASCOT
ELP 285

723 LONDON GRAYS TILBURY 723
720
FJJ 770

GREEN 720 LINE
BISHOPS STORTFORD
FJJ 642

Top, left: STL 2687 was one of the small number of the type in Green Line livery from 1946-49 (S. A. Newman). Top, right: The D type were of very basic speification, but performed yoeman service on the east London routes (Lens of Sutton). Bottom, left: T561 waits at Gravesend before its cross-London journey (P. Mitchell). Bottom, right: D146 shows off its painted radiator and small headlights at Brentwood (S. L. Poole).

Top, left: Despite its bus livery, TF53 has Green Line sideboards in this 1952 view on route 714 (A. B. Cross). Top, right: For many years stand-by coaches were kept in London to cover breakdowns. T639 shows the narrow blind which had nearly all possible destinations (A. B. Cross). Bottom, left: The LTC class saw occasional use on Green Line – LTC17 at Aldgate on 720 in March 1948 (A. B. Cross). Bottom, right: T543 found its way to Split Transport, Yugoslavia in 1954. It still carried L.T. red bus livery, and registration number but has acquired an off-side door. (D. W. K. Jones).

The experimental rebuilt RTC1 had many advanced features, but remained unique (Lens of Sutton).

RTC1 had a very unusual sliding door arrangement, seen on a busy summer-day in 1949 (A. B. Cross).

The revision was intended to bring into line fares on all forms of transport in the London Transport area. Green Line probably benefited most from some refinement of the previously rather coarse fare gradations; certainly passenger use increased from its pre-war level of 24 m. journeys a year to 27 m. in 1951 and 32 m. in 1953.

In the years immediately following the war, the mainstay of the fleet were the 10T10s, while the Qs were identified with the 715 route (Hertford and Guildford) 724 (High Wycombe—London) and 725 (Chesham—London) and the TFs worked from St. Albans, Luton and Dorking on routes 712, 713, 714 and 727 and later Grays. Double-deckers were virtually confined to the Aldgate group of routes. These services had been re-started with 37 new double-deck Daimlers with war-time utility bodies in Green Line livery from the Romford garage. The Daimlers were later augmented by another five transferred from Central Buses and several STLs but by 1950 the rather uncomfortable Daimlers were transferred to Central Buses and replaced by new double-deck RT's.

There had been some subtle changes. Destination indicators acquired their distinctive yellow and black colours (from 29 May 1946) and the side-boards were green with gold lettering. The livery was also simplified with Lincoln green becoming the main colour with less intricate relief and lining.

Having established the network, attention turned to the fleet. In view of the advancing age of some of the coaches, consideration was given to fleet replacement and the heavy peak-hour loadings again gave rise to consideration of double-deckers. The basis for an experiment was pre-war RT97, which had been used since the war in a series of 'pay-as-you-enter' experiments. This was not the now familiar one-man-operation but incorporated a seated conductor adjacent to the rear entrance. The experiments included three months on Green Line 721 but, not surprisingly, were not considered successful. The vehicle re-emerged in 1949 as RTC 1, a luxury coach seating 46 passengers. It was used on several routes but it was decided that (except for the intensive services on such routes as 721 and 722 where considerable experience had been built up with higher-capacity bus-type double-deckers) future rolling stock would be of single-deck type.

The advent of the modern underfloor engined, front-entranced vehicle was the most significant change in basic bus design for many years and the A.E.C. Regal Mk IV was chosen as the front-line Green Line coach for the fifties. No-one could have guessed that the type would be the mainstay of the Green Line system for more than 20 years from its introduction in 1951 with the last examples still running in 1979. The introduction was a fitting 21st birthday present for Green Line as it squared up to the exacting conditions of post-war days.

The first 25 RF type coaches were 27′ 6″ long vehicles for the central area private hire fleet and featured windows in the roof for improved visibility. The next 263 vehicles for service operation brought about a rapid transformation and ousted the older types, for

This rear view of RF281 on route 725 shows the classic lines of the class (R. F. Mack).

One of the RFs converted from Country buses to coaches at Windsor (G. Mead).

use on local bus services, very rapidly. These vehicles were to the full legal maximum length of 30 ft and were fitted with 39 well-upholstered seats, all but one facing forward.

The RF fleet on Green Line reached its zenith in 1956 when ten of the short private hire RFs, six central area and nineteen country area buses were converted to Green Line coaches. The red buses had air-operated doors fitted to conform to coach standards, whilst the country bus already had them. The 41 bus seats were reduced to 40 and slightly rearranged but these twenty-five vehicles never quite equalled their predecessors' internal standards.

It is interesting to compare the trend of the 1970's towards very high capacity one-man operated vehicles accommodating up to 100 passengers with the increased productivity which the RFs brought to Green Line. The T and Q coaches seated 30 to 34 and the RF allowed some 25% more passengers to be carried, which well suited the boom years of the early 1950's. However, driver and conductor operation was still the norm, which permitted the pre-war quality of service to be maintained. Many of the crews had been on coaches since the beginning and were justifiably proud of their position in the premier division of London Transport.

On the Romford based services the standard 56 seat RT double-decker had replaced the utility Daimlers in mid-1950. The only difference between these coaches and their bus cousins was the external livery, which featured a cast motif on the upper-deck side panels. Further examples of this type replaced single deckers on the 723/A/B in 1954.

The main feature of the 1950's was the passenger boom which restored Green Line's strong market position and enabled a stable and extensive network to be maintained. The development of the New Towns around London as overspill areas for the city's population created opportunities which produced some new coach services and changes to others. Harlow, Welwyn Garden City, Hatfield, Stevenage, Hemel Hempstead and Crawley were all planned to develop progressively over several years and have since outstripped their originally intended boundaries in most cases. This new traffic did much to help Green Line's development in the 1950's and 1960's.

The familiar Bell Punch tickets disappeared in 1954 in favour of the less attractive tickets issued from sturdy Setright machines. While the conductors must have welcomed the reduction in work, and the passengers no doubt missed the colourful old tickets, the demise of the most monotonous job of all—checking the individual clippings from a Bell Punch register for audit purposes—must have brought relief all round.

Most imaginative innovation of the period, and one which was a prelude to many later moves, was the introduction of the first orbital service, circling rather than crossing London. The 725 operated from Gravesend to Windsor via Dartford, Bexley, Croydon, Sutton, Kingston and Staines on an hourly frequency starting 1 July 1953. An instant success, it was only ten months before the service frequency was doubled between Dartford and Windsor to establish the basic

service pattern still operating in 1980.

The decade also brought its ups and downs: the Festival of Britain in 1951 and the Coronation in 1953 produced extra traffic, whilst the Suez crisis of 1956 saw services severely reduced for a while. The prototype Routemaster coach, CRL4, entered service in 1957 displaying many advanced design features and the future traffic Meccas of Heathrow and Gatwick Airports began their rapid development. But the end of the boom was not created by outside circumstances, but by the disastrous strike of all London Transport bus staff, which lasted for seven weeks from 5 May to 20 June 1958.

The London bus strike of 1958 was the worst single industrial dispute in the history of London's buses and coaches and caused passenger loss of unprecedented proportions. Unfortunately, this had to be reflected in service levels and the decade ended with the black clouds gathering.

Opposite: This interior view of an RF shows the extra length introduced by this class (L.T.E.). Top: RT4497 stands at Aldgate (G. Mead). Left: Prototype Routemaster CRL4 rounds Marble Arch en-route for Chertsey (R. F. Mack).

Until the early 1970's most Green Line coaches carried large sideboards giving comprehensive details of places served by the route. At first individual slip-boards were also used to give correct details where routes had alternative terminals. Orange and black were followed by green and gold, black and gold and finally yellow and black.

Production Routemaster RMC1454 weaves across Marble Arch on route 718 (Lens of Sutton)

727 EXPRESS
LONDON
LONDON EXPRESS 727
GREEN LINE
RF 239
MLL 776

713
LONDON
(BAKER STREET)
DORKING LONDON LUTON OR DUNSTABLE
RF 228
MLL 765

709 GODSTONE
709 CHESHAM LONDON CATERHAM 709
GREEN LINE
LYF 451

703 AMERSHAM
703 WROTHAM LONDON AMERSHAM 703
GREEN LINE
LUC 217

Top, left to right: RF239 on the short-lived Tring-London service 727 (G. Walker), standard RF228 on route 713 (Capital Transport), Blue blinds were used on the express section of 705-RF212 at Hammersmith (G. Walker). Bottom, left to right: Several experimental liveries were tried in the '60s as illustrated by RF100 (G. Walker), ex-private hire RF17 on route 703 complete with blinds in the roof-windows (P. J. Relf), another experimental livery was worn by RF271 in 1961 (G. Mead).

If two things could be said to summarise Green Line's problems in the 1960's, they would be service reductions and traffic congestion.

The London area probably suffered more from the new national prosperity than anywhere else in the Country. The private motor car became both the most desirable object to own and the prime cause of frustration for thousands. Traffic congestion had arrived and the authorities embarked on a massive programme of road building to by-pass bottlenecks and improve traffic flows. Fly-overs, underpasses and one-way systems caused major disruption while they were being built and were quickly choked up with the ever-increasing traffic. Running bus and coach services became a nightmare of uncertainty and the passengers started to lose patience with late running and lengthened journey times.

In 1962 the first new vehicles for 10 years arrived when 68 RMC type Routemaster coaches were delivered, symbolising a major policy change. These 57-seater double-deckers followed quite closely the prototype design, featuring well-spaced deep cushioned seats, platform doors, fluorescent lighting, overhead luggage racks and a brighter internal colour scheme. Mechanically they were fitted with the 9.6 litre engine, semi-automatic gearboxes and air-suspension. Unfortunately, since the order had been placed for these fine vehicles, passenger traffic had declined, and instead of providing much needed extra capacity for overloaded RF services, they were to herald reduced frequencies on some routes.

The twenty-minute service on 715 (Hertford-Guildford) was reduced to half-hourly, whilst 715A (Hertford-London) retained its same frequency when the first RMCs entered service on 29 August 1962.

716, 716A, 718, 719, 720 and 720A were all converted before January 1963 with 720 also suffering a reduced service. If it had been hoped that the new coaches would increase patronage, the actual results were not very promising.

23 August 1963 saw the start of a novel operation on 705, when the Windsor to London section of this long route to Sevenoaks was "expressed". Coaches ran over a faster route and only called at 13 stops

RT3606 (left) and RT4492 show front and rear of the standard Green Line RT (Lens of Sutton, A. B. Cross)

reducing the running time by 15 minutes, in a brave effort to improve passenger carryings.

The opening of the Dartford Tunnel in November 1963 saw the introduction of a disastrous extension of route 722 from Corbets Tey to Dartford. Passenger traffic was negligible over the new section and it is surprising that it was retained for 12 months.

Major changes were made in November 1964 which included a new service utilising the M1 Motorway. The 727 ran between Tring, Hemel Hempstead and London with only 19 stops. Again, this innovation was not successful and the route was withdrawn in October 1965. Other changes included a further "express" section on route 709 which ran via the A40 Western Avenue and some reshaping of several services.

The last new double-deck type used on Green Line arrived in mid-1965 with the 43 RCL coaches. Based on the RMC, these vehicles were 30 ft in length, (3 ft longer) and seated 65 passengers in similar comfort to the earlier Routemasters. They were intended to replace all the RTs on east London services and took over 721, 722, 723 and 723A in June and July. Because of their extra weight and length, heavier duty tyres were fitted which slightly increased the height and prevented RCLs from being used on 723B which passed below a low bridge at South Stifford. Hence the RCLs were allocated to Hertford for 715A releasing RMCs for Grays.

For some years there had been growing concern at the serious delays caused to cross-London services by traffic congestion, and the resultant inability to provide reliable departures from London for much of the day. The problem was tackled experimentally in two ways in November 1965—service 714 was simply split in half at Baker Street to provide two sections with theoretical connections, whilst 701 and 702 were split to provide an overlap in London (Ascot/Sunningdale—Victoria and Hammersmith — Gravesend). These experiments provided valuable information but were both discontinued; 714 in December 1966 and 701/2 in May 1968.

London Transport had announced their intention of trying a whole series of new vehicle types on bus and coach services before deciding on standards for the future. The first to arrive, and the only coaches, were 14 A.E.C. Reliances with 49-seat Willowbrook bodies to the new standard length of 36 ft. Classified RC these featured a new silver grey livery with broad Lincoln green band, yellow fleet names and sideboards. The specification also included luxury high backed seats, individual overhead ventilation, large picture windows and air suspension. They entered service on 28 November 1965 on the 705 service accompanied by extensive publicity.

At the same time RF136 was receiving a major restyling to up-date its appearance and comfort to obtain further service from the type. The result was an interesting new-look which was widely acclaimed. It entered service in March 1966 and a decision was quickly taken to carry out similar modifications to another 149 over the next few months. The Lincoln green and pale green colours were retained on the RF in a far more striking layout, but very attractively

RF136 looked like any other RF before it became the prototype for modernisation: left it stands at Addlestone (Lens of Sutton) and, right, on route 704 – note the round mudguards (G. Walker)

contrasted by the yellow fleetname, bullseyes and sideboards. The RC's were to adopt a similar colour scheme at repaint.

The second orbital route introduced on 10 July 1966 was very different. The 724 "orbited" north London but much further out than the 725, and introduced one-man operation to the coaches. It ran from High Wycombe to Romford via Watford, St. Albans, Hertford and Harlow, on a very limited stop basis serving only 25 major points. But one-man working was proved possible and plans began to be formulated for other conversions.

On the last day of 1966, in a large programme of service alterations, route 709 became a Monday to Friday peak-hour and Sunday only operation between Godstone and Baker Street and was converted to RCL operation. It was to remain in this unique form for a remarkable 13 years and was also to be the last double-deck service in 1976.

The almost unrelieved gloom of the last few years of the 1960's saw extensive service reductions and curtailments, following serious passenger decline. Fares also seemed to increase more often and more steeply, reflecting the scourge of recent years—inflation.

One of the most consistently successful Green Line services was introduced in May 1967 following months of careful research. Another orbital route, 727 also ventured to link for the first time the two major London Airports at Heathrow and Gatwick. Again limited stop, express, one-man operation was used and innovations included through booking with British Railways at Watford and Luton for air passengers. To cater for the anticipated influx of heavily laden customers, the modernised RF coaches had extra luggage racks fitted at the rear, which reduced seating to 35. The route was a great success and was to require extensive summer duplication in the following years. Always supported by high quality and profuse publicity, it pointed to the importance of airports in the future development of Green Line.

Meanwhile the RC coaches had failed to come up to expectation mechanically and they were laid up for many months. After repaint and fitment of luggage racks they re-appeared on 727 where the extra seats were most valuable, but the problems continued and they were quickly withdrawn.

Wholsale conversion of all single deck services to one-man operation occurred in November 1968 and February 1969 accompanied by considerable frequency and timetable changes.

The decade came to an end with sweeping political changes, fares increases and the withdrawal of all services on Christmas Day. For the first time coach crews could enjoy the day with their families!

RMC1468 at Hertford when new (P. Mitchell).

The RCs were allocated to Dartford for 725 duplication for a short time (B. E. Speller).

 RM1469 was altered as prototype for the later RCL class

The RCLs were longer than the RMCs – RCL2248 at Marble Arch (A. B. Cross)

Prototype CRL4 was extensively modified and became RMC4 (G. Mead).

Severe winter weather in 1969, but the services keeps running (J. G. S. Smith)

Rear view of RMC1500 at East Grinstead (P. J. Relf)

London stand-by coach RF80 performs a duty on route 704 (L. Akehurst).

London Country had to overcome an identity crisis on formation in 1970 and quickly adopted a new ''winged wheel'' logo. Said to represent the Company's area and fields, it was to be replaced after only a few years by the double-N symbol of the National Bus Company when corporate identity was adopted for all group companies.

Change, change and more change

Surburban coach SNC169 at Sevenoaks illustrates the Leyland National era on Green Line (C. Brinden)

". . .the property, rights and liabilities in question shall on vesting date be transferred to, and by virtue of this Act vest in, such company, being a wholly-owned subsidiary of the Bus Company, as the Bus Company may by notice published in the London Gazette designate for the purpose. . ."

This was the brief paragraph from the Transport (London) Act 1969 which brought about the most fundamental change in the basic organisation of Green Line since the original formation of London Transport in 1933. London Country Bus Services Ltd. was formed as a new wholly-owned subsidiary of the National Bus Company to take over the Country Bus and Green Line Coach operations of London Transport.

The change was hardly noticed by the travelling public, as the Green Line vehicles retained their distinctive livery and fleet names unaltered. Only the legal lettering was revised, to restore the famous "Bell Street, Reigate" address from which so much pioneering work had emanated.

The new Company had to come to grips with two basic problems. Firstly, it was undercapitalised and operating at a serious loss from the first day of its existence and, secondly, the fleet handed over by London Transport was largely outdated. The financial problem was not new: London Transport had been losing money on the 'green' operations for some years and L.C.B.S. has continued to suffer from the interconnected problems caused by inflation and declining patronage ever since. In only two of the last ten years has income met basic operating costs.

The fleet replacement crisis was tackled promptly by the ordering of 90 A.E.C. Reliance coaches with 36 ft long 45-seat Park Royal bodies. These coaches, classified RP, were to replace the Routemaster double deck coaches and facilitate the completion of the one-man operation programme. However, it was almost two years before the first arrived during which time major changes were few.

The general trend of the late 60s, of reducing frequencies, minor withdrawals and fares increases continued. Route 710 became a slightly unusual operation in February 1971 when it was shortened to operate from Amersham to Uxbridge only, unsuccessfully as it turned out as the complete demise of the route followed only eighteen months later. On the other hand 727 became a three airport service when it was extended into United Counties territory from Luton Station to Luton Airport in March 1971, and Routes 704 and 705 were extended into Alder Valley territory at Windsor Safari Park on Summer Sundays from July 1971. 724 abandoned High Wycombe and Amersham in favour of Heathrow Airport and Staines in 1972.

New Year's Day 1972 marked the beginning of the wholesale introduction of the new RPs and the conversion of busy east London routes 721 and 723 to one-man operation. This move would have been inconceivable in earlier days, but had become essential. 723 received the ill-fated RC coaches; their mechanical novelties had proved unreliable and they had spent some time on services 711, 725 and 727, but never found an acceptable home.

The O.M.O. conversion programme with new RPs proceeded apace with 718 succumbing in February, 704, 705 and 716/A in March and 715/A in April. This left the peak hour only 709 as the one remaining double deck crew-operated service.

The vehicle problems referred to earlier were by no means cured by the 90 RPs and some surplus vehicles from other National Bus Companies were acquired to assist. The only ones allocated to Green Line were 21 A.E.C. Swifts with unusual Alexander 45-seat bodies originally intended for South Wales Transport and classified SMA. Their AH505 engines were rather underpowered for coach work but they had several unusual features. The bodies had ramped floors and very large windows which gave all passengers excellent visibility. The green used for the exterior was a lighter "Tilling" shade which was to become the new fleet standard until N.B.C. green took over. Finally the rear destination indicators were below, rather than above the back window giving a rather unexpected appearance. They were also the last coaches to have rear blinds at all!

The SMA class which was introduced in March 1972 spent their entire coach life of less than seven years on south London orbital route 725 (and later 726) from Windsor, Dartford and Northfleet garages, except for one which was allocated to Crawley for excursion and other coaching work. At the end of 1979 most SMAs had been withdrawn and sold, although some remained on bus and contract work.

In 1972 replacement of the twenty-two-year-old RF coaches was becoming urgent, and the advent of the Leyland National type promised to provide a worthy successor, after extensive research and development programmes. Unfortunately, the standard bus version was chosen for Green Line use with very upright and unyielding PVC covered seats. Apparently, it had proved impossible to obtain any concessions from the standard production line model, although the appearance of a "suburban coach" version in 1974 proved that there was no technical reason for the decision.

What the passengers on Route 721 thought in February 1973 when their year-old RP coaches were replaced by the first LNCs is not recorded. Undoubtedly the advent of the new green and white National dual-purpose livery produced a very attractive exterior but the interior was hardly welcoming to the longer distance rider.

The introduction of the first Leyland Nationals in 1973 produced a series of reallocations (LNCs on to 721, 711 and the Tring allocation of 706; RPs to 720 and 724) which was to be a feature of the remainder of the 1970s. Later Leyland Nationals were to the shorter 10.3 metre length (LNCs were 11.3 metres long) and interim improvements included a moquette covering to the standard bus seats before the full suburban coach version arrived. The Leyland National, however, was never the success on Green Line which had been hoped. Perhaps it was unreasonable to expect a basically high capacity urban bus design to meet the unusual requirements of Green Line and no-one will regret the decision which was made in 1976 to upgrade the vehicle image of the service. But before we turn to the recent upturn in the fortunes of the famous marque, there was a further period of problems.

1974 and 1975 saw a continuing series of service reductions culminating in the sudden and complete withdrawal of 701 on 3 October 1975. Inflation was

Last of the famous RF class still performing in 1979 (G. Brigden).

RCL2237 was the only one to receive new NBC livery & fleetnames (G. Walker)

SMA6 on a rare visit to route 705 (G. Brigden).

The edible coach? RP46 in all-over advertisement livery (J. G. S. Smith).

RPs served on Route 721 for a few months when new. RP18 at Aldgate (S. Clennell)

raging and all the problems which had started in 1970 were coming together. The mixed vehicle fleet, the lack of adequate central overhaul facilities, outdated garage maintenance services, and the acute national shortage of spare parts caused serious unreliability. The old image of Green Line took a few hard knocks.

Fortunately another new phenomenon was on the scene, in the form of County Council revenue support. The Local Government Act had given the Counties the responsibility of co-ordinating all transport facilities and the power to keep unremunerative services operating by making revenue support grants. A complicated system of submissions and consultation now exists to ensure that all sections of the community have a say in their local transport services and the level of support given. The different Counties show very different attitudes and have demonstrated the complex relationships which the modern world has introduced into bus operation.

However, Green Line's renaissance has been possible only by virtue of the revenue support which is given to many routes.

In 1976 London Country decided that the whole Green Line operation required a major overhaul to fit it for the new situation of the late 70s and 80s. Most important was the order for 30 new coaches each year to full luxury specification to transform the somewhat motley collection of vehicles then running. These coaches were to be rented for a period of five years, so a total of 150 was planned. This was later increased to 180. The first 150 coaches are British Leyland Reliances with the large AH760 engine giving ample power without stress. The first 60 coaches have been fitted with Telma electric retarders to overcome braking problems, but subsequent deliveries have had self-adjusting brakes as a more economical improvement. The bodies have been split between Britain's two major luxury coach builders Duple and Plaxton, with Duple providing 90 (classified RB) and Plaxton 60 (RS). Livery features the now standard green and white, but applied in a very striking manner.

The cessation of production of the Reliance has left a void which (at the time of writing) has yet to be filled. Two British Volvo B58 coaches with Duple bodies and

RP52 pick-up passengers at Addlestone having lost its motif (L. Norris collection)

The SMA class looked very attractive in N.B.C. dual-purpose livery (G. Brigden).

two Leyland Leopards are due to enter service in Spring 1980 on a one year trial and future vehicle policy will be watched with interest.

The first five of the new coaches were introduced on 29 January 1977 coincident with major revisions to the Luton—St. Albans—London—Dorking services. This clearly set the pattern of the next few years. Poorly used sections of route were to be sacrificed in favour of speed, new destinations and strong marketing. The old 712, 713 and 714 were replaced to the north of London by new services 707 and 717. Both operated from Luton Airport to London, Victoria with less stops, improved running time; 717 had the added distinction of being the first Green Line to serve Brent Cross near Hendon, which had developed into a major regional shopping centre.

Marketing techniques first used in this introduction included widespread door-to-door leaflet distribution, press advertising, posters and extensive public relations back-up. And the change was an immediate success. Passengers clearly appreciated the improvements and traffic to Brent Cross, particularly, was excellent.

On 2 April 1977 a number of important changes was introduced which confirmed that some cuts were still necessary to account for falling demand. Long established sections of 718 (Walthamstow-Victoria), 720 (Buckhurst Hill—Aldgate) and 706 (Croydon-Chelsham) disappeared entirely whilst some major restructuring introduced some novel operations.

New services 702 and 703 were introduced between Bishops Stortford and Walthamstow or Waltham Cross respectively. Between Bishops Stortford and Epping the new routes replaced most buses plus Green Line 718 and 720, creating a hybrid type—is it a low grade coach or a high grade bus service? However, another comprehensive marketing campaign emphasising the excellent connections on the Victoria Line at Walthamstow Central created some remarkable passenger loads in the first few weeks.

The 706 was mainly replaced by a revised service on route 708 between East Grinstead and Aylesbury, but the previous importance of the main road between

RF221 in N.B.C. bus livery on Route 725 in 1977 (G.Brigden).

GREEN LINE
716 A WOKING
JPA 126K

GREEN LINE
716 LONDON
JPA 154K

LONDON COUNTRY BUS AND COACH ENQUIRIES SOUTHD
LONDON COUNTRY

LONDON COUN
708
HEMEL HEMPSTEAD
GREEN LINE
GREEN LINE
TPD 172M

Top, left to right: RP26 splashes through floods at Welham Green in 1974 (J. G. S. Smith), a number of RPs were refurbished in 1978/79. RP54 skirts a reservoir near Walton (G. Brigden), long Leyland National LNC51 on Route 706 at Victoria (S. Clennell). Bottom, left to right: Despite being repainted in bus livery, RP74 was running on Route 727 at Crawley (Lens of Sutton), SNC72's attractive exterior concealed on ordinary bus interior (S. Clennell), passengers board RB22 on Route 726 at Heathrow Airport Central Bus Station (G. Brigden).

Croydon and London was seriously declining and Chelsham lost its coach allocation.

Another novelty in these changes was the replacement of a section of London Transport red bus route by a Green Line coach. 215 was cut back from Cobham to Esher and 715 deserted its old haunt of that famous arterial road, the Kingston-by-pass, to run via Hampton Court to Kingston.

The Kingston By-pass did not lose its Green Line service completely as a new peak-hour commuter special is now provided by 710. This fast link to and from London also utilises the new Ripley By-pass and stops at main points only.

The final change in April was the extension of 724 to Windsor via Staines, Runnymede, Old Windsor and Datchet. The other end of the route was cut back to St. Edwards Way in Romford instead of the station and the allocation changed from Romford to Harlow garage. Romford garage's daily service requirement dropped to only six coaches; a pitiful reflection of its glorious past.

The next red-letter day in the 1977 Green Line diary came on May 21 when a substantial increase in vehicles required occurred for the first time in many years.

Route 700 was launched with quite a blaze of publicity as a Silver Jubilee year link between Victoria and Royal Windsor running nonstop via the M4 in only 50 minutes. An hourly service gives the crowds of visitors a fine link cutting 40 minutes off the normal 704 times. The first three RB coaches made their debut from Windsor garage adorned with special stickers, to mark the Queen's silver jubilee.

The long established 704 and 705 finally achieved the obvious diversion into Heathrow Airport Central after carefully avoiding this major passenger objective ever since the central area complex was opened twenty years before.

New service 726 was formed by the rerouting of alternative 725s between Ashford and Windsor via Ashford, Heathrow Airport and the M4 motorway to Windsor. An hourly service thus links whole areas of South London direct to Heathrow for the first time.

The success of existing airport links was confirmed by the augmentation of the 727 to half-hourly between Crawley and Heathrow. In 1977 this operated in the Summer only, but became a year-round service from 1978. Delivery of RS and RB vehicles was so far behind that few of these changes were introduced with new coaches, but publicity was extensive.

On 1 July 1977 the axe finally fell on 721 and Romford Garage, thus ending the Hillman connection. Railway electrification, traffic congestion and inflation had killed off the busiest-ever Green Line service.

In October 1977, 711 was withdrawn, being partly replaced by new service 790 between Amersham, High Wycombe and London and bus 422 between Sutton and Reigate. The former was advertised in conjunction with the frequent Oxford-London services of City of Oxford and tickets became interchangeable. So, the pattern was set. 1978 and 1979 saw more sweeping changes and the rapid introduction of new vehicles on most services.

The Great North Road service 716 was swept away in favour of speeded-up 722 and 732 with the latter again including Brent Cross which provided valuable extra traffic. The first refurbished and overhauled RPs appeared on these services pending delivery of RS coaches.

Wrotham suffered another change of route after many previous alterations, but this time the new 729 service ran in peak hours only and was extended to the Maidstone & District depot at Borough Green. The long-established special operations for race meetings at Brands Hatch were renumbered 739.

Further changes were made to the Harlow based services in May 1978 and the Windsor-London-Sevenoaks—Tunbridge Wells services were extensively reshaped. The new 701 route featured a lengthy section on the M4 Motorway to reduce running times particularly to Heathrow, while the more historic aerodrome at Biggin Hill lost all but its Sunday coach service (apart from specials for the annual air displays).

Cross-London operation ended in 1979 with 704 splitting in May, 715 in October and 719 being curtailed.

The growing importance of the Airport traffics again manifested itself with an entirely new type of Green Line service which started on 28 April 1979. Christened "Jetlink 747", with no particular similarities to the ubiquitous Jumbo Jet, an hourly non-stop schedule between Heathrow and Gatwick was launched with massive international marketing. The coaches feature a special yellow, greeen and white livery and the route name appears on both sides and back. After six months, more than 45,000 passengers had been carried at the premium fare of £2.50 single. The luggage problem is catered for by the use of the rear boots and passengers are set down at the terminal of their choice at Heathrow.

October 1979 saw another new service, and it was the long awaited sister of the 725—an inner orbital service across north London. The concept had been discussed for years, but it was not until Green Line's 49th year that agreement and support were available. The 734 runs from Hertford to Addlestone via Enfield, Wood Green, Muswell Hill, Golders Green, Brent Cross, Wembley, Ealing, Hounslow, Heathrow Airport and Staines on an hourly frequency. A two-year trial is assured and 200,000 households received a leaflet through their door to maximise public awareness.

With planning for the 50th anniversary of Green Line well under way at the end of 1979, 1980 promised to continue the improvements of recent years. Green Line is therefore going into the 1980s with every prospect of many more years of operation, and showing every sign of creating as much interest for the historian as ever.

Right: RC1 descends Reigate Hill on Route 711 (B. J. Davis). Opposite: "Suburban Coach" SNC147 demonstrates its ability to close half the door to conserve heat at terminals (Lens of Sutton)

711
HIGH WYCOMBE
VIA LONDON
(OXFORD CIRCUS)
GREEN LINE
GREEN LINE
PAY AS YOU ENTER
PLEASE
LEYLAND
NATIONAL
GPD 298N
HE 51
SNC147
COACHES
LNC

To establish the private hire business several attractive leaflets and advertisements were produced. After many years in which the business was allowed to contract, Green Line is regaining a major foothold in this lucrative business.

Private hire, excursions and express

The only private hire TF to survive the war, TF9, follows RF19 on a private hire outing in the early '50s (Lens of Sutton).

As related in Chapter 1, East Surrey was quickly off the mark in the excursion field after the war of 1914-18. The services continued to prosper during the twenties, and by 1930 Arthur Hawkins had twelve coaches designed primarily for this duty—six Associated Daimler 419 type coaches with glass front and side-screens and a folding canvas roof dating from 1927, and six sunshine-roof coaches on a more advanced A.E.C. Regal chassis. These latter elegant vehicles were delivered in April 1930.

The L.G.O.C., too, had developed the excursion and tours business, with Hampton Court, Windsor and the Thames riverside generally as obvious attractions to the visitor. It used similar vehicles to the earlier East Surrey coaches—A.E.C. Y and B types completely open to the weather except for the heavy canvas hood and side screens which could be erected by two men (preferably more) in about as long as it took for the average shower to blow over.

When both East Surrey and L.G.O.C. moved tentatively into the Express Coach business, they turned initially to their private hire stock to provide the vehicles: East Surrey to operate the 419s in 1928-29 between Reigate, Redhill and London; L.G.O.C. with its trial service of October 1929 between Watford and Golders Green, using ten of its A.D.C. 416A coaches. The first of the A.E.C. Reliance fleet with similar canvas-roof bodies followed on the initial Watford to London service.

Following the formation of Green Line Coaches Ltd. in July 1930, it was decided to put all the private hire coaches into Green Line livery, though L.G.O.C. retained centralised control of the greater part of the fleet and continued to operate it mainly from a garage at Brixton Hill, South London. This apparent anomaly did not hinder the free interchange of vehicles as traffic demanded, however, and in the years 1930-1935 particularly, the Central Private Hire fleet performed a valuable back-up service to the regular Green Line operations. One instance has already been quoted (Chap. 6): the drafting of perhaps half-a-dozen private hire vehicles to clear the Whipsnade Zoo traffic on a fine Sunday evening. The reverse could be seen, too, on Derby Day, when many an L.G.C.S. bus or coach found itself on the way to Epsom Downs with an "On Hire" slip in the front

Top, left to right: An L.T. guide points out the sights from a TF (L.T.E.), ex-Hillman's LT1429 with a party at Wembley Stadium (J. F. Higham), handsome T363 came from West Herts Coach Company (D. W. K. Jones). Bottom, left to right: Almost all of the 34 Reliances of the 1932 private hire fleet were at Victoria to meet a party (L.T.E.), Green Line coaches from the service fleet were used to operate local excursions – TF52 from Grays (D. A. Jones) and T523 from Romford (L. Norris collection).

GREEN LINE
VATE
LT 1429
EV 7340

LONDON TRANSPORT

LONDON TRANSPORT
TOUR
FROM ROMFORD
T 523
ELP 247

LONDON TRANSPORT
TOUR
FROM GRAYS
FJJ 663

PRIVATE
To HIRE A BUS or COACH
LUC 202
EGO 519

LONDON TRANSPORT
EXCURSION TO
EPSOM RACES
GREEN LINE
MLL 816
518
MLL 515

EXCURSION
EPSOM RACES
JPA 114K
GREEN LINE

052
BOURNEMOUTH
WINCHESTER SOUTHAMPTON
GREEN LINE
SPK 204M

window to cover its movements.

The London Passenger Transport Act of 1933 gave no powers to the new Board to operate outside its boundaries, as laid down in the Act. This curbed the former East Surrey tours business drastically, as it was cut off from the South Coast and the most lucrative part of the operation. Not until 1970 was this restriction removed by which time many other coach operators had secured extensive express and excursion licences covering almost every conceivable destination. By contrast, the Central London private hire business continued to grow during the thirties, so that it was able to absorb most of the non-standard coaches of various makes and specifications which were then being acquired in ones and twos from the smaller independent operators. Some of these were to a high standard of luxury, others less so, and within limits they enabled a wide range of needs to be met. Most of the coaches concerned are mentioned in appendix d.

The Reliances and some of the less-suitable members of the fleet were withdrawn from private hire during 1935. In replacement, some of the ex-East Surrey Regals and four Regal saloon coaches acquired from Lewis Omnibus Co. of Watford were allocated to Private Hire, with other acquired vehicles of varying degrees of suitability for the purpose. These were four Dennis Arrows from Red Rover (DL36-39); a total of six Dennis Lancets (2 from Puttergill's Golden Arrow undertaking (DT4 & 5); two from Imperial of Romford (DL34-35, later DT6 &7); and one each from Gravesend & District (DT 1) and Penn Bus Co. (DT 9). There was also DST 6, a Daimler from West London; the Albion Valiant (AN 1) from Sunset Pullman; the Renown six-wheeler (LT1429) of Hillman; an ex-Maidstone & District Gilford (GF160) and lastly the small Bedford coach (BD 23) which was the contribution of Sunshine Saloons of Kingston.

Top, left: Prewar LTC15 contrasts with RF2 at Camberwell Garage (D. W. K. Jones). Top, right: These RFs have not been put out to grass, but rest while their passengers watch the Derby (A. B. Cross). Bottom, left: A few years later RP14 had sunnier weather for its visit to Epsom (S. Clennell). Bottom, right: P4 leaves Crawley Bus Station on National Express service O52, one of several now operated by Green Line (J. G. S. Smith).

Recourse to hiring was necessary on occasions until the advent in 1937 of the 24 purpose-built 6-wheel LTC type with 30-seat Weymann bodies and petrol engines—the last for London service. Two years later came the 12 TF type with observation panels in the roofs of their Park Royal bodies. Of the observation roof TFs only TF 9 survived the bombing of 1940, and could be seen on "Seeing London" tours for some years after the War.

The LTCs soldiered on in the post-war years, even being pressed into service as Central buses on occasions during vehicle shortages of 1947-49. In 1951, however, came RF 1-25, 27± 6² long against the 30± of the standard Green Line coach, and with observation panels in the roof, public address system and other refinements. They marked a break with Green Line identity in that they appeared in a striking green and grey livery, with the London Transport fleet name in red, and no reference to Green Line. The RFs were followed by 15 8 ft. wide vehicles designated RFW type, a rather unusual design of Eastern Coachworks bodies, without destination indicators, as they were intended for special private party work. Thus the fleet was standardised for a number of years, until a change of policy brought in hiring of coaches under contract from independents to relieve pressure on the business caused by staff shortages. Meanwhile the Country Area operations had continued on a reduced scale with some of the RFs and RFWs allocated to Country Garages. Other local coach work was covered by normal buses and coaches, including modest excursion programmes to well-known venues in the London area.

With the formation of London Country Bus Services, Ltd., in 1970 the shackles of the London Transport "special" area were finally shaken off, and the ensuing years have been devoted to rebuilding a thriving coaching business in several distinct areas.

Delivery of the first purpose-built touring coaches was delayed until 1973 when five Plaxton 49-seat A.E.C. Reliances were delivered during the late Summer. These featured the new all-over white 'National' coach livery and were allocated to five different garages around the area to develop excursion and private hire work. Most promising area was Redhill/Reigate/Crawley where the acquisition of Southdown licences in 1972, along with some local bus services, had provided a sound base. For the first two seasons a Southdown Leyland Leopard with Harrington coach body was borrowed pending delivery of the new coaches.

Reorganisation of National Travel's London area operations and the transfer of Gravesend area services from Maidstone & District to London Country in 1977/78 brought the second real opportunity for expansion with a greatly enlarged excursion network covering much of South East London and the first regular commitment to the National Express network; albeit only during Summer months. At the same time the decision was taken to market all the Company's coaching activities under the famous 'Green Line' banner, and the coach fleet reappeared in the distinctive white and green livery. Further coaches were acquired in 1978 and 1979 from National Travel (all AEC Reliances with either Plaxton or Duple coach bodies) bringing the operational fleet to 17. Future plans envisage the use of a number of each new batch of Green Line coaches for their first few months' operation on private hire, excursion and express services, thus releasing the current mixed fleet for sale, and ensuring new vehicles are constantly available.

It is thus possible to see Green Line back in the coastal towns of the South where East Surrey pioneered express services so many years ago. They are also regular visitors much further afield in Bournemouth, Exeter and Paignton on regular duplication for National Travel (South West), and in the North for National Travel (East).

These developments have not been without setback, and excursion programmes from Hertfordshire and Essex have failed to gain the public support necessary to achieve success. Even as this book goes to press, Government proposals to remove all licensing controls from excursions and express services could significantly alter the balance of operations—but Green Line is ready and able to take advantage of the changes.

Badges have always been a means of identification and Green Line staff have had a variety over the years. The familiar P.S.V. Badge is a legal requirement, but the operator's own badges, usually bright metal and green enamel, form an interesting study in their own right.

Green Line operated from many make-shift garages in the early days. This was in London Road, Guildford, and shows routine maintenance being done in the open (L.T.E.).

Left: An RF stands in Tunbridge Wells Coach Station (L.T.E.). Bottom, left to right: Staines Garage was hastily constructed and provided more facilities than some (L.T.E.), some garages had very rudimentary parking areas (L. Norris collection), while High Street Garage, Ongar had mud, ex-Autocar and East Surrey Regals and an ex-L.G.O.C. Reliance (L.T.E.).

At the time of the early expansion of Green Line services in 1929 to 1931, garages were opened for the purpose of housing coaches for the newly-introduced services. Many were small, some were improvised, one or two were just open yards. Most closed when more permanent accommodation could be found, usually in new or extended Country Bus garages. The following list may not be exhaustive, but it gives an indication of the extent of this activity.

Opening Date:

2.10.29	Watford, Leavesden Road (Code AL).
20. 4.30	Slough, Alpha Street (Code BL).
10. 7.30	Staines, London Road (Code CL).
17. 7.30	Guildford, Rice & Harper, London Road (Code DL).
23. 7.30	Romford, Metcalf's Works (Code EL).
2. 8.30	Maidenhead, Grenfell Road.
17. 9.30	Welwyn, Jenner Parsons Ltd.
20. 9.30	Harpenden, Comfy Cars, Luton Road.
11.10.30	Addlestone, Weymann's Bodies Ltd.
31. 1.31	Sunbury, Hanworth Road.
7. 2.31	Southall (in A.E.C. works).
18. 2.31	Aylesbury, Cubitt Works.

2. 3.31 Gidea Park, 988 Hare Street
21. 5.31 Brixton, Effra Road

The codes AL, BL, etc., did not survive for long. No external garage codes were then carried by Green Line coaches until London Transport extended the Central Area garage coding to the Country Department and Green Line in December 1934. Codes then and subsequently allocated are as follows:

AM	Amersham (later MA)
BT *	Brixton (LT Private Hire)
CM x	Chelsham
CY x	Crawley
DG	Dunton Green
DS	Dorking
DT	Dartford
EG x	East Grinstead
EP *	Epping
GD x	Godstone
GF	Guildford
GR	Garston (renamed Watford in 1979)
GY	Grays
HA	Harlow
HA *•	Harefield
HE *	High Wycombe (HW at first)
HF	Hatfield
HG	Hertford
HH	Hemel Hempstead
HN *	Hitchin
HW*	High Wycombe (later HE)
LH x	Leatherhead
LS *	Luton
MA	Amersham (AM at first)
NF	Northfleet
RE *	Romford (London Road)
RF *	Romford (North Street)
RG	Reigate
SA	St Albans
SJ	Swanley
SL •*	Slough (Langley Road)
ST	Staines
SU *	Slough (Bath Road)
SV	Stevenage
TG *	Tring
TW*	Tunbridge Wells
WA*	Watford High Street (WG at first)
WC	Windsor "Coach" (later WR)
WE*	Ware (People's)
WR*	Ware (Town Hall)
WR	Windsor (WC at first)
WT*	Watford (Leavesden Road)
WY	Addlestone
WG*	Watford High Street (later WA)

* Since closed.
• No Green Line coaches allocated.
x No longer operate Green Line coach services.

The coach operations of 29 companies as listed below were incorporated into the Green Line network in the short period between 1930 and 1935, most being absorbed in anticipation of, or following, setting up of the London Passenger Transport Board in 1933. The major concern, Green Line Coaches Ltd., with its associates, brought in 446 coaches, but in total there were nearly 650 vehicles to be dealt with. The routes they had worked needed to be rationalised to eliminate overlapping and duplication of services and to permit the withdrawal of elderly and unfit vehicles of a variety of makes.

Acme Pullman Services Ltd.
Amersham & District Motor Bus & Haulage Co. Ltd.
Associated Coaches (Ongar) Ltd. (Forest King).
Autocar Services Ltd.
Battens (Amalgamated Omnibus Services and Supplies Ltd.)
Beaumont-Safeway.
Blue Belle Motors Ltd.
Bucks Expresses (Watford) Ltd.
East Surrey Traction Co. Ltd.
Edward Hillman's Saloon Coaches Ltd.
Fleet Transport Services Ltd.
Green Line Coaches Ltd.
Lewis' Cream Line Coaches.
Maidstone & District Motor Services Ltd. (part only, including former Redcar Services Ltd. Tunbridge Wells route).
National Omnibus & Transport Co. Ltd.
Premier Line Ltd.
Premier Omnibus Co. (Watford) Ltd. (West Herts. Motor Services).
Price's Super Coaches.
Queen Line Coaches Ltd. (Baldock Motor Transport).
Red Rover Saloon Coaches (Cain).
Regent Motor Service.
St. Albans & District Motor Services (Russett).
Skylark Motor Coach Co. Ltd.
Strawhatter Motor Services (Hill).
Sunset Pullman Coaches Ltd.
Sunshine Saloons (Sunbury-Kingston).
Tilbury Coaching Services Ltd.
Upminster Services Ltd.
West London Coaches.

Makes of Coaches Involved
377 vehicles of A.E.C. and Associated Daimler origin (7 main types).
186 Gilfords of 5 main types.
58 Leylands of 3 main types.
Small numbers (6 or less) of the following makes:- Albion, Bedford, Daimler, Dennis, G.M.C., Guy, Maudslay, Morris, Saurer, Thornycroft and Tilling-Stevens.
Total numbers fluctuated as some vehicles were condemned before others had been acquired and many vehicles (mainly Gilford and Leyland) were transferred from coach to bus operation and vice versa.

The workshops at Reigate in 1934, where the flood of acquired Gilford coaches was rehabilitated, repaired, condemned or cannibalised. (H. Snook).

BUCKS EXPRESS

Specially designed to mark the Golden Jubilee of Green Line, this logo is being used extensively on vehicles, publicity, stationary and merchandise during 1980.

Publicity

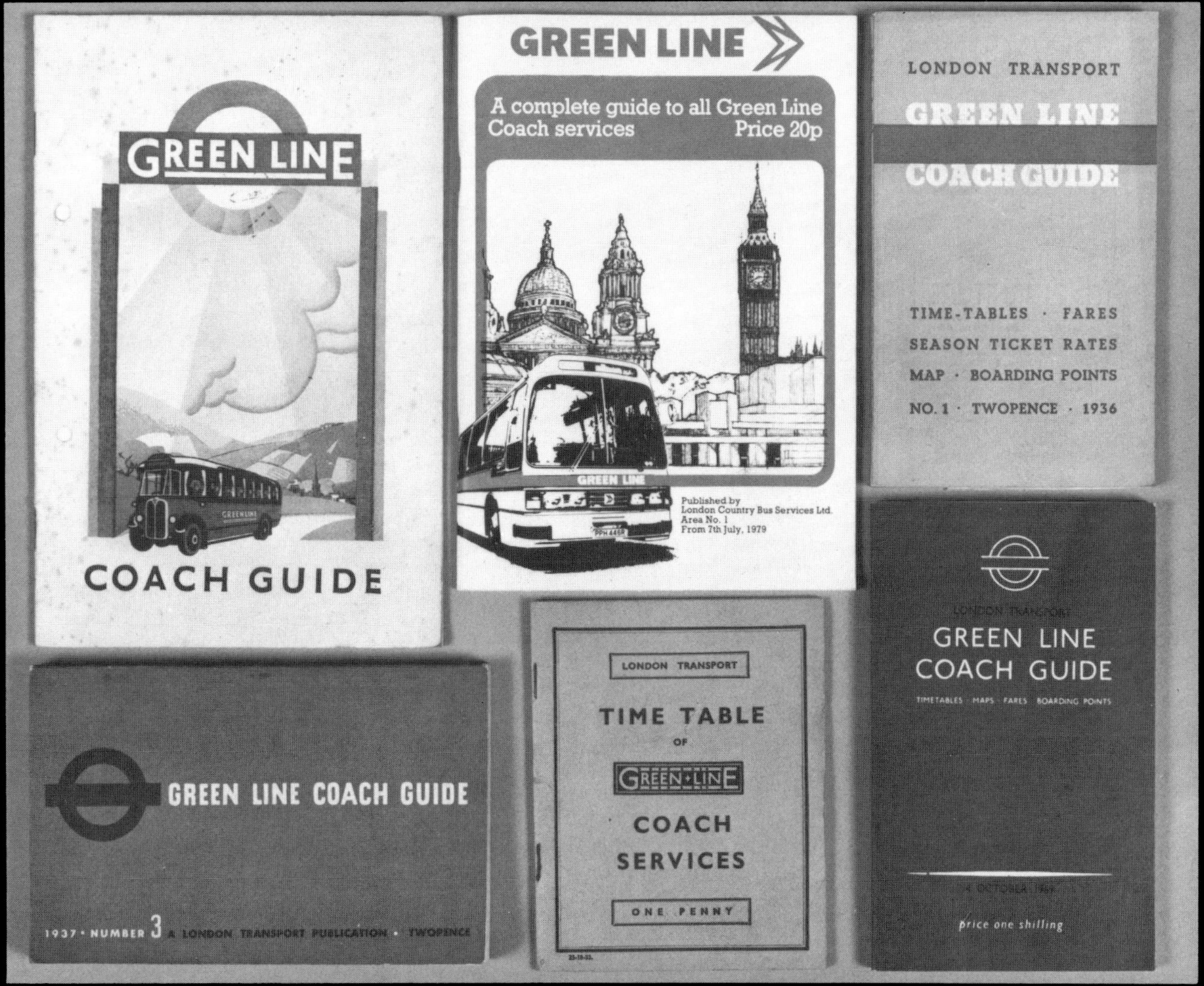

Publicity for Green Line services has always been prolific. Throughout the years the timetable has been the most important piece of publicity. Six examples are shown here: – Left upper – the original 1931 book which never went on sale, probably because its contents were out of date before completion. Centre upper – the new coach guide re-introduced in 1979. Right upper – 1936 guide in upright style. Left lower – 1937 guide in landscape style. Centre lower – 1933 guide in same style as bus timetables of the period. Right lower – last guide produced by London Transport in 1969.

Above – the route map has been produced in several different styles, but always in a pocket size. Latest editions combine coach services with the bus network, a practice tried in the mid 1960's but not perpetuated. There is also a separate coach map produced as part of a comprehensive travel guide leaflet. Poster versions have also been produced over the years for display throughout the area. Right – as companies were absorbed in the early 1930's many individual timetable leflets were produced by Green Line in their standard style, but with the previous operators' names. On formation of the LPTB in 1933 many were overprinted as shown.

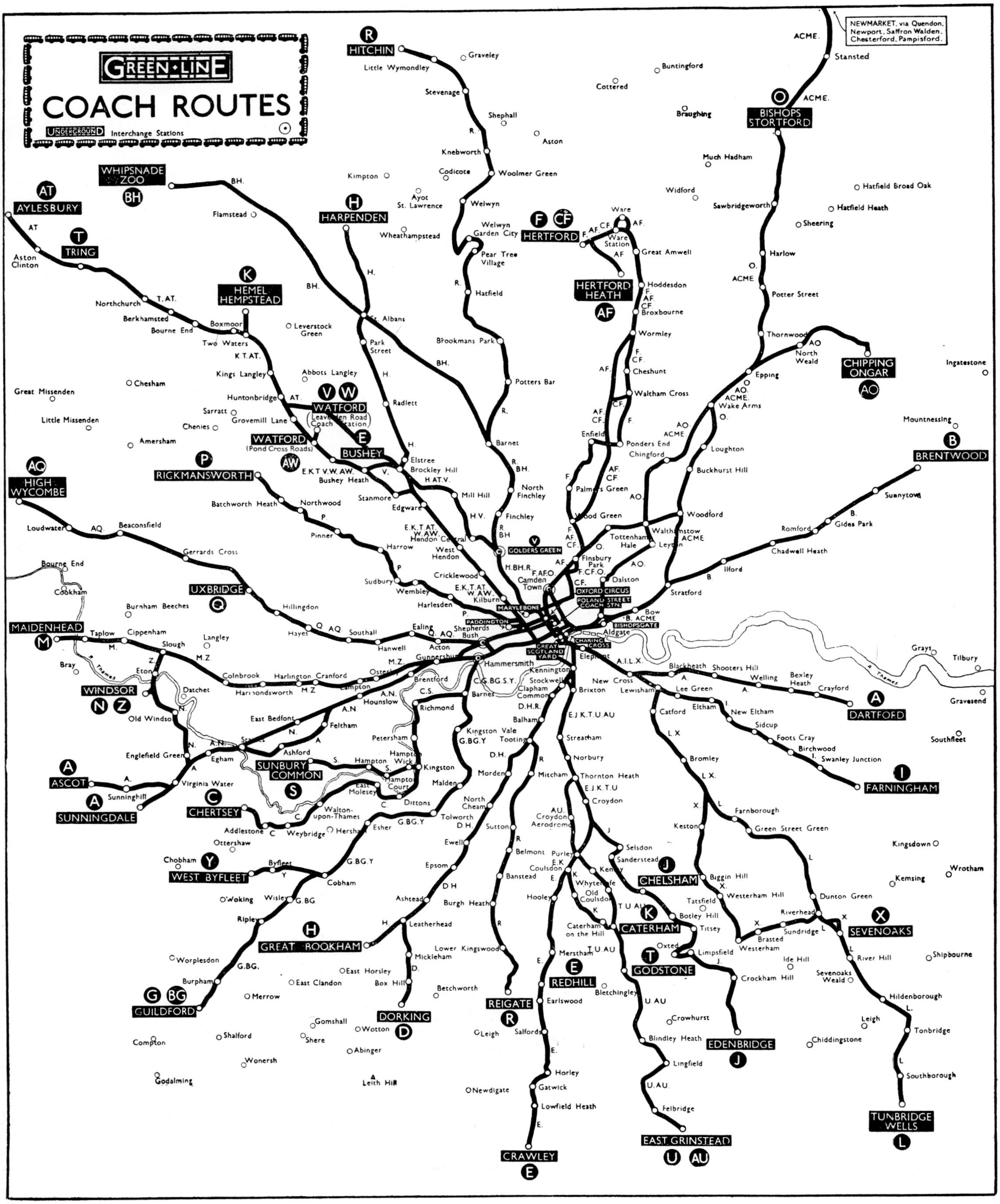

This 1933 map is reproduced in the full size of the original leaflet. It shows how many of the basic routes introduced in the pioneer days are still operating today.

GREEN LINE
LONDON
ROUTE L
TUNBRIDGE WELLS
Daily Every 30 Minutes
ROUTE X
SEVENOAKS
Daily Every 60 Minutes
GREEN LINE
ROUTE AU
EAST GRINSTEAD & LONDON
DAILY
Every 60 Minutes
GREEN LINE
ROUTE A
ASCOT SUNNINGDALE LONDON DARTFORD & GRAVESEND
EVERY 60 MINUTES
GREEN LINE
ROUTE J
WATFORD LONDON & REIGATE
ROUTES A AND AA
ROUTE A GRAVESEND, DARTFORD, LONDON & ASCOT
ROUTE AA GRAVESEND, DARTFORD, LONDON & SUNNINGDALE
ROUTES A AND AA
ROUTE A GRAVESEND, DARTFORD, LONDON AND ASCOT
ROUTE AA GRAVESEND, DARTFORD, LONDON AND SUNNINGDALE
ROUTES A & AA
ASCOT SUNNINGDALE AND LONDON AND GRAVESEND
Time-table and particulars from February, 1935
GREEN LINE ROUTE W TIME TABLE
Ongar Epping London
On and after September 1, 1937
GREEN LINE TIMETABLE
ROUTES E, F: Edenbridge or Tatsfield Chelsham, London, Hemel Hempstead or Aylesbury
GREEN LINE COACHES
now running daily
Except H2 temporarily postponed
GREEN LINE COACH ROUTE 708
HEMEL HEMPSTEAD LONDON AND EAST GRINSTEAD
On and after October 2, 1946
GREEN LINE COACHES
ROUTE 704
Tunbridge Wells London and Windsor
ROUTE 705
Sevenoaks London and Windsor
GREEN LINE COACHES
ROUTE 703
WROTHAM LONDON AMERSHAM
On and after June 11 1949
ROUTE 725
GRAVESEND BROMLEY · CROYDON WINDSOR
Starting on July 1, 1953
GREEN LINE
LONDON TRANSPORT
GREEN LINE COACH ROUTE 715·715A
TIMETABLE AND FARES
Starting on August 8, 1956
GREEN LINE
COACH ROUTES
721-722
TIMETABLE AND FARES
(Summer 1965)
GREEN LINE COACH
714
TIMES AND FARES
DORKING
Leatherhead
Kingston
LONDON, Victoria
From 29 January 1977
LONDON COUNTRY
707·717 737 EXPRESS
LUTON AIRPORT
LUTON
ST. ALBANS
BRENT CROSS or BARNET
GOLDERS GREEN
OXFORD STREET
VICTORIA
WHIPSNADE ZOO
M1 MOTORWAY
HENDON
GOLDERS GREEN
OXFORD STREET
VICTORIA
TIMES & FARES
From 21 MAY 1977
GREEN LINE
GREEN LINE
700, 701, 704.
Windsor Safari Park, Windsor, Slough, Heathrow Airport, Hammersmith, London.
TRAVEL
734
GREEN LINE
Welcome to Britain
A guide to coach services from Heathrow
GREEN LINE
734

Opposite – the evolution of the individual timetable leaflets for each route is illustrated from the early simple style, some on coloured paper, to the attractive leaflets of today. The second leaflet from the left in the centre row details the first wartime re-introduction with an overprint indicating how the situation changed rapidly.
Left upper – a selection of recent publicity, which caters far more for tourists, airports and specialist markets than earlier material.
Left lower – in the mid 1970's the Green Line map was produced in several languages for distribution overseas.

Abbreviated details of registration numbers.

Early vehicles carried a wide variety of registration numbers, largely because of their diverse origins. Full information is available from the specialist societies, so pre-1936 vehicles are not listed here:

T403-452	CLX551-575, CXX151-175
T453-718	ELP177-289, EYK201-353
LTC1-24	EGO505-528
Q81-105	CGJ186-210
Q186-187	CLE127-128
Q188	DGO500
Q189-238	CXX382-406, DGX220-244
TF1-88	DYL904, FJJ603-618, 629-674, 761-777, FXT41-48
D67-9, 71, 73	GYE56-58, 60, 62
D133-7, 141, 143-9, 151-4	HGC260-264, 268, 270-276, 278-281
D156-9, 161, 164-70, 172-9	HGC283-286, 288, 291-297, 299, HGF800-806
RT97/RTC1	FXT272
RT600/1/5/10/3/20/35/8/50	HLX417/8/22/7/30/7, JXC443/6/58
RT967/8/74/9/99, 1021, 2252	JXC495/6, JXN2/7/27/49, KGU181
RT3224-3259, 3438, 4489-4509	KYY953-970, LLU601-618, LYR857, OLD709-719
RT3604-6/9/12/6/20/4/35/47/56	MLL914-6/9/22, MXX131/5/9/50/62/71
RF26-288	LYF377-476, MLL513-612, MLL763-825
RF289-294	MLL926-931
RF295-313	NLE514-532
RF1-25	LUC201-225
RFW1-15	LUC376-390
Lightweights	NLP635, PHW918, PTE592
CRL4/RMC4	SLT59
RMC1453-1520	453-520CLT
RCL2218-2260	CUV218-260C
RC1-14	CUV59-72C
RP1-90	JPA101-190K

SNC71-97, 99-102, 104-112	TPD171-195M, UPE196-197M, UPE199-202M, UPE204-212M
SNC116-140	WPG216-225M, XPD226-227N, GPD294N, XPD229-240N
SNC141-177	GPD295N, XPD242-244N, GPD296-298N, HPF298-327N
SNC178-202	LPB178-202P
RS1-15	PPH431-441R, TPD12S, PPH443R, TPD14-15S
RB16-30	PPH446-451R, TPD22-30S
RS31-45	VPH31-36S, XPK37T, VPH38-40S, XPK41-45T
RB46-52	VPH46S, XPK47-48T, VPH49-50S, XPK51-52T
RB53-60	VPH53S, XPK54-56T, VPH57S, XPK58T, VPH59S, XPK60T
RB61-105	YPL61-105T
RS106-120	APM106-120T
RB121-135	EPH121-135V
RS136-150	EPH136-150V

Hertford Garage deck area with two Gilfords and a Q undergoing attention (L.T.E.).

A.D.C. 419 and A.E.C. Reliance coaches at Effra Road, Brixton in 1931 (E. G. P. Masterman)

R6 is another Reliance (E. G. P. Masterman).

To keep presentation relatively simple, the composition of the fleet is dealt with in three parts—Part 1 covers the standard types acquired or delivered in the early years, Part 2 covers the non-standard types acquired, and Part 3 the fleet from 1936 onward, when acquisitions had ceased. For completeness, Part 1 includes the vehicles used by East Surrey and L.G.O.C. before the formation of Green Line Coaches Ltd. in July 1930, and vehicles provided by Autocar Services Ltd. which did not become the property of London Transport as on 1 July 1933 ownership of Autocar Services was transferred to Maidstone & District Motor Services.

Reference is made throughout these lists to the London Transport classification codes which enabled different chassis and body types to be easily identified. Details of the full meaning of these codes can be found in specialist publications.

Part 1: Early standard types, acquired or new

A.D.C. 416A Type (Total 10):
These ten Associated Daimler coaches were new to L.G.O.C. in 1928 for Private Hire and carried 28-seat bodies in an attractive light green and cream livery. When the trial service between Golders Green and Watford was introduced in Oct. 1929, (at the end of the summer season) these vehicles were available to start the service. In 1930 an exchange took place whereby all ten of these chassis passed to National. All the bodies remained with Private Hire, however, five of them being mounted on Reliance chassis which had formerly seen service as National buses, and the other five being given entirely new Reliance chassis.

A.D.C. 419 and 427 Types (Total 41):
The 419 Type coaches when new in 1927 had 26-seat open canvas-roofed bodies and Daimler engines. L.G.O.C. possessed 33 (five of which were operated by National for a time) and East Surrey had six all for tours and excursions. At a later date, about 1930, the L.G.O.C. vehicles were rebuilt with front bulkhead carrying a standard destination indicator, a rear dome in aluminium and glazed side windows. Thus up-dated, they became a useful reserve for the expanding regular coach services, and were frequently to be seen acting as duplicates or even service coaches in times of pressure. All received standard Green Line livery and were not withdrawn until after the 1933 season.

The two 427 saloons were quite massively built for a seating capacity of only 18 on a normal-control chassis. New in 1928, they were seen occasionally as duplicates before being relegated to bus duties in 1930 as AD 54 and 55 in the National fleet.

R 1—34 (Total 34):
The Reliance chassis were new in 1929 and 1930, and formed the backbone of the L.G.O.C. Private Hire fleet at that time. Their semi-saloon bodies, retained the opening canvas centre section, rendered them equally suitable, by the standards of the time, for the emergent regular coach services. Thus it was that when L.G.O.C. opened up Watford—Charing Cross and resumed operation between Watford and Golders Green in the winter of 1929 the first twenty Reliance

The prototype Green Line Regal, T38, at Golders Green (D. W. K. Jones)

The perfect 1930 design – T150? (D. W. K. Jones).

coaches were employed until such time as the standard A.E.C. Regal T-type coaches became available. Designated R-type, there were eventually 34 of this useful pattern of coach, 25 from L.G.O.C. and 9 from National (Nine more saloons, R35-43, came from Battens in 1933, as is related later). All wore Green Line livery. The Reliances received standard front destination indicators at about the time they entered regular express service, but were otherwise unaltered until 1935. Four had been sold to Holtspur Coaches in 1933. During 1935 the remaining 30 Reliances were withdrawn from coach duties and fitted with new all-metal bus bodies to augment the Country bus fleet. In this new capacity they served until 1938, when the chassis were finally condemned and the metal bodies were transferred to T-type coach chassis then being released from service by the advent of newer vehicles.

T 38, T51-149, T155, T157-206 (Total 151):
1930 marked the advent of the A.E.C. Regal T-type coaches which were to be the mainstay of the coach fleet for so many years.
T 38 had a prototype body built at Chiswick and mounted on one of the chassis intended for the buses of the T 1-50 series (Class 1T1). Entering service between Watford and Golders Green in January 1930, it had a 28-seat rear-entrance body which differed from the production run in details such as the window and emergency exit arrangements.
The next 150 were 27-seat rear-entrance vehicles with bodies by L.G.O.C., Short Bros. or Hall Lewis, Class 7T7. They retained their 6-cyl. petrol engines until withdrawn. 40 were delivered in General red and black livery (including T38); 17 were East Surrey coaches (T52, 66, 72, 73, 81, 82, 85, 90, 91, 100, 102, 103, 110, 113, 116, 117, 118); nine were allocated to Autocar (T 65, 70, 77, 86, 88, 98, 106, 109, 112). The ramainder bore Green Line livery from the start. Five of the General coaches were transferred to Amersham and District in 1931 and operated the London-Chesham route in Amersham colours until 1933 (T 69, 71, 89, 96, 104).
All were withdrawn from coach service in 1938-39 on the advent of the new 10T10 type, but some were converted to service vehicles or saw country bus service during the War. These were taken by the War Department for the movement of displaced persons in Germany immediately after the War ended.

T 150-154 (Total 5):
These were petrol engined private hire coaches of the L.G.O.C., with all-weather 32-seat bodies, classified 8T8, delivered in 1930. Although they acquired full Green Line livery, they were rarely seen on regular coach routes, and were withdrawn in 1938.

T207-306 (Total 100):
The second batch of Regal coaches had 30-seat front-entrance bodies, 50 by Duple and 25 each by Ransomes and Weymann. Internally their appointments were similar to the earlier batch, but they had a sliding door for entry and the emergency door was at the rear instead of on the offside. The class (1/7T7/1) were delivered between December 1930 and March 1931. Three (T 216, 274 and 305) were experimentally fitted with A.E.C. Acro oil engines, later exchanged for the successful A.E.C. Ricardo 8.8 litre oil engines. In 1931, these three were the first oil-engined coaches in the London area, and were attached to the L.G.O.C. Hanwell Garage for servicing.

In April 1933 T 232 had its body replaced by a new and stylish all-metal design by M.C.W. No other body of this design was built, though it probably provided data for the all-metal coach bodies fitted in 1935 to other Regals absorbed from Blue Belle and Queen Line Coaches, whose original bodies were ageing rapidly.

Survivors of the T 207-306 batch of coaches were still to be found on Central and Country bus duties after the War, though with oil engines, 26 of them with all-metal bus bodies from Reliance R-type which had been scrapped (reclassified 11T11).

From mid-1931 a number of the standard Regals bore the type letters ET instead of T. This signified their allocation to East Surrey stock for working former East Surrey and Autocar routes. The distinction disappeared in 1933.

T 219 is preserved in the London Transport Museum at Covent Garden.

LT 1137 (Total 1):

This was an experimental 6-wheel double-deck coach which commenced service on the busy route E (Bushey-Redhill) in September 1931. The chassis was an A.E.C. Renown from a series of L.G.O.C. single-deck buses and the body, built at Chiswick, had a sunshine roof, 50 seats, a *front* entrance and a *rear* staircase. The design was elegant but did not prove satisfactory in service, and after rebuilding with a stairway near the front entrance LT 1137 entered Country Bus service from Hatfield Garage. It was finally withdrawn in 1946.

Q1 (Total 1):

The later 4Q4 and 6Q6 types owed a lot to Q1, (class 1Q1), which was an experimental single-deck A.E.C. petrol side-engined 37-seat bus introduced by the L.G.O.C. in September 1932. It has a place here because it worked on coach duties from Reigate for some months in 1933, and eventually became a Country Area bus.

T307-358, T 391-402 (renumbered) (Total 52):

Between January 1932 and July 1933 Green Line allotted fleet numbers to vehicles acquired or operated in conjunction with other concerns. Thus certain A.E.C. Regals were given numbers between T 307 and T 358.

Top: Backbone of the fleet – the 7T7s as illustrated by T251 (D. W. K. Jones). Right: The magnificent double deck Renown coach LT1137 (L.T.E.).

Top; The prototype Q, after transfer to the Country area, at Reigate (H. F. Adcock). Left: The sun-roof Regals of East Surrey were used to cope with the expansion of 1932/3. T317 became T401 later (J. F. Higham).

T 307-8 came from Bucks Express, absorbed in February 1932 and had Dodson bodies generally similar to the Green Line series T 207-306, and were classified 1/7T7/1. T 309-24 from the East Surrey fleet were used in regular service from January 1932 to meet vehicle shortages. T 325-45 were allotted to Autocar Services coaches, but this group never came into London Transport stock, as on 1 July 1933 Autocar and its fleet were transferred to Maidstone & District Motor Services. T 309-45 had 29-seat Hall Lewis bodies with sun roofs. There were two distinct designs, some having a full canopy over the cab and bonnet, and a roof luggage rack, others —the earlier ones—lacking both features, e.g. T 309-314 of the East Surrey group: Classification was 8T8/1 and 8T8/2. T 346-51 came from Blue Belle Motors in July 1932 and with bodies built by London Lorries seating 31. T 352-57 came from Queen Line Coaches in April 1933 with 31-seat London Lorries bodies. T 346-57 were rebodied in October 1935 with new 26-seat front-entrance M.C.W. bus bodies. They were nevertheless often seen on Green Line duty until 1939, and took the classification 5T4 after rebodying. T 358 was taken over with Aston of Watford's fleet in May 1933. It had a 30-seat Strachan body, and was classed 1/8T8/3.

In 1935 T 307-318 of the above group were renumbered T 391-402 in the same order, their original numbers having been allotted to 12 Central buses acquired from Thomas Tilling.

All this group had standard A.E.C. 6-cyl. petrol engines during their career as coaches.

T 359-368 (Total 10):

In late 1933 London Transport absorbed Amersham & District and the Lewis (Watford) concern, and the coaches acquired were turned over to Green Line as T 359-368:-

T 359, 361, 362, 364, 365 and 366 came from Amersham & District and had 32-seat Strachan bodies and petrol engines; classified 1/8T8/3, they remained on coach duties until 1938 when four were rebodied as buses and T 365/6 were sold.

T 360, 363, 367 and 368, ex Lewis, being non-standard vehicles, were transferred to the Central Area Private Hire Department where they remained until sold in 1938-39. They had Harrington bodies. It is perhaps interesting to note that when London Transport hired private coaches to relieve an acute shortage of vehicles in 1948-49, one of those utilised

Ex-Amersham & District T366 (D. W. K. Jones).

was the former T 363, still going strong in the ownership of Paddington Transport Co.

Part 2: Non-standard types absorbed from independent operators.

A.E.C. (Total 10):
(9 Reliance and 1 Renown). The 9 Reliance coaches were from Batten (Amalgamated Omnibus Services and Supplies Ltd.). They were numbered R 35-43 and were used almost indiscriminately as buses or coaches before being withdrawn about 1937. The Renown was the six-wheeled luxury coach from Edward Hillman, which was transferred to Private Hire duties and numbered LT 1429. It had a 32 seat Harrington body.

Leyland:
From 1932-1934 Green Line created an L series to accommodate all its acquired Leyland vehicles, the total reaching 47 coaches of Lion, Tiger, and Titan models. Under London Transport in 1935 a new TR series brought together all Tiger vehicles, bus or coach, and there was a similiar TD series for Titans. L 1-3 were Lions, L 1 being a 26 seat saloon new in 1927 to Invicta Transport at Biddenden, Kent, the other two had 32 seat all-weather bodies, new in 1929. All three came from Associated Coaches (Ongar) Ltd. and were withdrawn prior to the renumbering by London Transport of all other vehicles in the L series into the TD & TR classes.
TD 132 and TD 174-191: These 19 coaches were all originally Premier Line vehicles. It was unusual to find a Titan as a single-deck chassis, and this was probably in the interests of standardisation with the Premier bus fleet. These stoutly built coaches had Duple bodies on TD1 chassis and saw service until 1937-38.
TR 2-5 and 18-31 were Premier Line Tiger TS 3s which had a spell on bus work before being returned to Green Line service, again until 1937-38. TR 8 came from Chiltern and was transferred to the Private Hire fleet. TR 9 and 10 were TS 1s new in 1931 to Aston of Watford. TR 6, 11-17 came from Maidstone and District, and had a varied career as relief coaches or as buses. TR 32-35 were excursions and tours coaches owned by Prince Omnibus Co. They were very well-appointed and tended to appear on both Green Line service and Private Hire for a while. Later fitted with

LT1429 only carried its fleet-number on the off-side (D. W. K. Jones).

standard route boxes, they were in regular Green Line service until about 1938. TR 36-40: These were 5 coaches originally bought by Redcar for their Tunbridge Wells—London service, and acquired by Maidstone and District when they absorbed Redcar in 1935, becoming Maidstone Nos. 700-704. As a result of re-organisation in 1935, the London service was taken over by London Transport, and with it the 5 Tigers. After a spell in Maidstone colours but with Green Line transfers added, they were repainted and became TR 36-40. These Beadle bodied 25-seat vehicles were lively for their age, and shared with other Redcar coaches the peculiarity of having single tyres at the rear. With the rest of the Tigers, they lasted until 1937 or 1938.

Gilford (GF type):
Although 186 of the 220 Gilfords acquired by London Transport were designated coaches by their former owners, nothing like that number ran as Green Line coaches at any one time, the bulk being gradually drafted to the bus fleet and frequently used as Green Line relief vehicles in times of pressure.

Ex-Premier Line Tiger TR3c at Windsor in 1935 (J. F. Higham).

GF103 came from Tilbury Coaching Services (J. F. Higham).

The first series consisted of the Gilford coaches taken over or controlled by Green Line Coaches Ltd. prior to 1 July 1933, plus the two Cream Line coaches:-
GF 1-18 ex Skylark (19 acquired; one not numbered), GF 19-22 ex Regent, GF 23 ex GF 19 (Regent) re-numbered, GF 24-28 ex Bucks Express, GF 29-35 ex Associated Coaches, GF 36-49 ex Acme, GF 50-51 ex Cream Line.
Only 6 of the above remained as coaches to be embodied in the second series initiated by Green Line in 1934:-
GF 1-3 ex Super Coaches, GF 4-5, 36-68, 107-125 ex Hillman, GF 6-21, 24, 27, 29-32, 34-35 and 69-73 ex Upminster Services, GF 22-23 ex Regent (from first series), GF 25-26 and 28 ex Bucks Express (from first series), GF 33 ex Associated Coaches (from first series), GF 74-76 ex West London, GF 77-88 ex Sunset Pullman, GF 89-101 ex Strawhatter Coaches, GF 102 ex Fleet, GF 103-106 ex Tilbury Coaching.
Some of the vehicles taken over from the companies listed above went straight to operation as buses; others followed and a few were withdrawn, leaving gaps in the list.
Finally, in 1935 London Transport's comprehensive

new numbering scheme placed all the Gilfords then designated as buses on the end of the coach list, i.e. from GF 126 upwards. Buses were given the suffix 'B' and coaches 'C', but the distinction was less clearly observed in practice. Vehicles continued to be transferred from 'C' to 'B' category, but this seemed to mean little. In truth, the existence of a large pool of Gilfords which could by their design be turned over at will from bus to coach duty helped to tide over the shortage of vehicles that prevailed until 1936; anything that would run, be it designated bus or coach, would be pressed into service at peak weekends.

Albion:
One Albion Valiant coach with 31 seat Duple body was acquired from Sunset Pullman, and after a short spell on Green Line service was drafted to Private Hire work as AN1c.

Bedford:
One Bedford of Sunshine Saloons became a Private Hire coach as BD 23.

Commer:
Two 18 seat Commer 6TK Invaders from East Surrey saw brief Green Line service before being transferred to bus duties.

Daimler:
The two Daimler coaches were vastly different in character. One, a 1931 CH6 type with Duple 32 seat body acquired from West London Coaches, became DST6 in the Private Hire fleet. The other, on a 423 type chassis, with 20-st. body by Short Bros., was introduced by L.G.O.C. in 1927 as a coach for private parties with a high standard of appointments. It later saw Private Hire service in Green Line livery, but was little used after 1934. It is thought to have survived to be designated PR 1 in 1935.

Dennis:
Five Dennis coaches were acquired from Red Rover. Four Arrows, two with Birch bodies and two with Thurgood continued to be used for a while on the erstwhile Red Rover London-Aylesbury service and later were used for private hire. Green Line classified them as D 1 and D 3-5, an older EV type coach being D 2. London Transport's 1935 re-numbering gave the

Top, left to right: This Albion Valiant from Sunset Pullman coaches became AN1c (D. W. K. Jones), one of the newest members of the HIllman's fleet, became GF122 (D. W. K. Jones), ex-Red Rover DL38 at a Wembley Cup Final (D. W. K. Jones). Bottom, left to right: Smallest member of the private hire fleet was Bedford BD23 (D. W. K. Jones), ex-East Surrey GMC coach MT6523 (D. W. K. Jones), the sole Daimler CH6 acquired by Green Line became DST6 (D. W. K. Jones).

GREEN LINE
GF 122
LONDON TRANSPORT

PRIVATE
PRIVATE
DL 38
LONDON TRANSPORT
GT 1564

PRIVATE
DST 6
GP 689

West London's larger Saurer was XY5337 (D. W. K. Jones).

Ex-Maidstone & District Tilling Stevens Express B10A after withdrawal (D. W. K. Jones)

Arrows the numbers DL 36-39, the EV being withdrawn after bus service.

G.M.C.
This was a 20-seat sun-roof coach originating with East Surrey as their No. 67. It received Green Line livery but was sold out of service by 1936.

Guy:
An old 20-seat coach came from Beaumont-Safeway. It is thought that two 32-seat vehicles of G.W.R. origin may have been designated G1/2. None saw more than brief service with London Transport in any capacity.

Maudslay:
There were 5 ML3-type coaches, three from Bucks Express and two originating with the G.W.R. The class was designated M1-5 by Green Line: they were withdrawn by 1935.

Morris:
Two Morris Viceroy coaches came from the East Surrey fleet came via London General Country Services to the Green Line Private Hire fleet, and were designated MS 10 and 11 in 1935, by which time they were on Country Bus duties.

Saurer:
This Swiss make was unusual in London coach use, though the L.G.O.C. had had at least one in the 1920's. Green Line acquired two elderly all-weather examples when West London Coaches was absorbed; they were withdrawn about 1934.

Thornycroft:
Three Thornycroft BC/F coaches with Vickers 22-seat bodies originated with the G.W.R. in 1929. They survived to be designated TH 1-3, and to receive full Green Line livery, but were quickly sold.

Tilling Stevens:
The six coaches acquired were "Express" type of 1927/28 vintage. Two were absorbed with West London Coaches; they ran for a while on their original route, but mainly as reliefs operating from Amersham Garage. After some bus work, they were withdrawn in 1935. The other four coaches all had canvas roofs, and came from Maidstone and District; none is believed to have survived to be repainted in Green Line colours, but they did see some service from Tunbridge Wells on route L, with Green Line stickers covering the Maidstone insignia. In 1934 they were sold.

Part 3: New Vehicles 1935-1979

T 403-452 (Total 50):
The first development in the vehicle replacement programme was the 9T9 class of 50 30-seat Weymann bodied coaches which entered service in 1936, They had a 7.7 litre oil engine, fluid transmission and a pre-selective 4-speed gearbox, and servo-assisted hydraulic brakes. They were converted to ambulances at the outbreak of war, but many saw post-war service as buses up to 1952. T 448 is preserved by Mr. Donald Allmey.

Q189-238 (Total 50):
The 'Q' was an unorthodox A.E.C. design in which the engine was placed on the offside of the chassis behind the driver, thus increasing passenger space. In

Still new 9T9 stands in the sun on Reigate Garage forecourt (H. F. Adcock).

GREEN LINE
BYFLEET
LONDON
GREEN LINE
Q228c
GREEN LINE
DGX 234

HEINZ
TOMATO KETCHUP
SWAN
VESTAS
GREEN LINE
SUNNINGDALE
LONDON
GRAVESEND
GREEN LINE

PRIVATE
LONDON TRANSPORT

PRIVATE
GREEN LINE
DGO 500

Top, left to right: Standard Q228 shows clearly the location of the engine (J. F. Higham), one of the 27 4Q4 buses converted for coach service (L. Norris collection), most numerous class was the 10T10 illustrated by T506 at Reigate (P. Mitchell). Bottom, left to right: The three-tone green pre-war livery suited the LTC class (D. W. K Jones), Q188 worked mainly as a bus from Hertford (L.T.E.), the dramatic driver's cab made TF1c a sensation when new (D. W. K. Jones).

fact, a longitudinal seat was placed literally over the engine. Other distinctive features of the design were the long wheelbase and the single rear tyres. The 6Q6 class was designed for Green Line work, with Park Royal bodywork seating 32. Heating was provided, and the dummy radiator grille served as an air intake. The roof line was higher than in bus versions and an attractive appearance was achieved. After ambulance duties during the War the Qs returned to coach duties for a while, mostly ending as buses round about 1952.

Q 81-105, 186 & 187 (Total 27):
The 4Q4 type was the standard Country Area bus, new in 1935 with 35-seat B.R.C.W. bodies to replace many of the miscellaneous acquired vehicles. Twenty-seven were switched to coach use in 1937 after being fitted with luggage racks and interior heating for passenger comfort, while externally sideboards and the dummy radiator grille in the full-width front panel were added. They were reclassified 1/4Q4/1. Before the War these vehicles had reverted to bus duties, with the exceptions of Q100 which did not revert until 1948. Q83 is preserved by Mr Bill Cottrell.

Q188 (Total 1):
The final 'Q' was an experimental 6-wheel chassis with centre-entrance double-deck Park Royal body, designed for Green Line service and classified 7Q7. It had hydraulic transmission and an electrically-operated gearbox. In 1936 it was in some respects ahead of its time; it was not found suitable for coach operation and such service as it saw was from Hertford Garage on bus routes and its working life ended early in the War.

LTC 1-24 (Total 24):
These ruggedly handsome A.E.C. Renown coaches were specially built for the Private Hire fleet, with Weymann 30-seat bodies, new in 1937. After the War they helped out from time to time on Green Line coach & Central bus services before being sold in 1951.

T 453-718 (Total 266):
These 266 A.E.C. Regals gave sterling service from their introduction in 1938 until the War, when they were converted into ambulances or saw service directly with the U.S. Army or as 'Clubmobiles' for the U.S. Forces. Completely rehabilitated after war duties, they

continued as first-line coaches until 1952; a fine record. They were more powerful than the 9T9 version, having an 8.8 litre oil engine. There was a ducted heating and ventilation system. The first batch of 150 had 30-seat Chiswick built bodies and were classified 10T10, while the remainder seated 34 and were classified 1/10T10/1. T499 was a 33 seater and was classified 1/10T10/2.
Many of the 10T10s were sold to local transport undertakings in Yugoslavia and elsewhere overseas, together with a few 9T9s and 6Q6s. They performed a valuable role for several years more. Some were adapted for passenger loading on the right-hand side, in other places the back (emergency) exit sufficed.
T 504 is preserved by the London Bus Preservation Group.

TF 1-88 (Total 88):
The last of the pre-war standard types was technically advanced in both chassis and body design. The TFs were the first purpose-built design in Britain to have an under-floor mounted engine, while the body and chassis were of integral construction, that is, forming a single unit of great strength with some savings in weight compared with the then-customary separate units bolted together.
The TF chassis had an 8.6 litre Leyland engine developing 94 b.h.p., which drove through a fluid flywheel and pre-selective gearbox provided by A.E.C. Gear changing and braking were operated by compressed air, a rotary compressor being provided. A ducted fresh-air ventilating system utilised heat from the main engine radiator, which was placed at the nearside of the driver's cab. The design was the result of collaboration between engineers of Leyland Motors and London Transport, and utilised standard Leyland units wherever possible.
An outstanding feature of the body was the excellent visibility for the driver. The prototype, TF 1, classified 1TF1, which went into service at the end of 1937 with a Park Royal body, employed a most unorthodox cab design, later modified to bring it into line with the production model. 75 of these (TF14-88), classified 2TF2, were at work in 1939, and had 34-seat bodies built at Chiswick.
The remaining twelve of the total of 88 chassis (TF 2-13), classified 2TF3, received Park Royal bodies with observation panels in the roofs, and were

Right: STL1506 was used on Green Line service during the war (D. W. K. Jones). Bottom: A standard TF on Route 723 (Lens of Sutton).

Left: Utility Daimler shares Aldgate, Minories with a Trolleybus and TF (A. B. Cross). Bottom: RT97 during its brief service on Route 721 (A. B. Cross).

These were part of an order for 50 Daimler CWA6 chassis with STL type engines, with 56-seat bodies by Duple. They were delivered in Green Line livery at Romford Garage in March 1946 for use on routes 721 and 722.

D 67, 68, 69, 71, 73 (Total 5):
Five other Central Area Daimler CWA6s with Brush bodies were repainted in green and transferred to Romford garage in December 1948, replacing five STLs.

RTC 1 (RT 97) (Total 1):
The basis of this double-deck coach was an A.E.C. Regent III (RT 97) which had been used for a 'Pay as You Enter' experiment. This included three months on Green Line service 721 before withdrawal. Between 1946 and 1949 RT 97 was completely rebuilt in Chiswick Works and emerged as RTC 1, specially designed for Green Line operation, with luxury seating for 46 passengers, power-operated sliding door at the rear, an elaborate heating and cooling system and fluorescent lighting. Trials followed on 704 and other routes, but events overtook RTC 1 when a

intended for private hire and tours. Their life was short, however, as all but TF 9 were destroyed by a bomb on their garage at Peckham in 1940.
After conversion to ambulances during the war, the TF's resumed coach duties in 1946 and were withdrawn from coach work during 1952. TF77 is preserved by London Transport.

STL Types (Total about 180):
When Green Line operations were re-introduced on a limited scale during the War years, some older coaches were brought out of store. After the blitz had died down, heavy traffic grew up on certain routes, and the main services were provided by about 180 STL-type double-deck buses transferred from the Central bus fleet and painted green, together with some Country Area STLs.
Ten STLs (2522/3/8, 2548/9, 2553/9, 2607, 2625 & 2637) carried Green Line livery between 1946/49 for use on East London services. They were standard LPTB 56-seat examples.

D 133-7, 141, 143-9, 151-4, 156-9, 161, 164-70, 172-9 (Total 37):

COUNTRY
GREEN LINE
704 TUNBRIDGE WELLS
PAY AS YOU ENTER PLEASE
LYF 427
PAY AS YOU ENTER PLEASE

Opposite: Modernised RF76 at Windsor (Lens of Sutton). Top: RT3234 leaves Aldgate on Route 721 (C. Carter). Left: RF69 clears a queue at Victoria (J. H. Aston).

decision was taken that, apart from the heavy commuter traffic on routes 721 and 722, new replacements would all be single-deck vehicles. After withdrawal, RTC 1 continued to render useful service as a development vehicle for interior heater experiments.

RT 600/1/5/10/3/20/35/ 8/50, 967/8/74/9/99, 1021, 2252, 3224-3259, 3438, 3604-6/9/12/6/20/4/35/47/56, 4489-4509 (Total 85):
To replace the Daimler double-deckers, 36 of an order for 56-seat standard RT-type double-deckers were allocated to Green Line in 1950. These were exactly similar to the London bus version, except for the fact that no advertisements were displayed and the upper panels carried a 'Green Line' motif in relief. 12 more were allocated in 1952/3 and a further 21 were delivered to Grays in 1954 for route 723. The group of 16 RTs numbered between 600 and 2252 were painted in Green Line livery for relief duties in 1960. Later versions had the upper deck bullseye motif as a transfer, but all were classified 3RT8/1. RTs were replaced on the East London services by the Routemaster, but those used on relief duties continued until the late 60s.

RF 26-288 (Total 263):
The post-war replacement for the entire fleet of single-deck coaches was the RF type, on A.E.C. Regal Mark IV chassis. They were classified 2RF2/1. Advantage was taken of new legislation to put a 30 ft. long body on a 2-axle chassis and so increase the number of seats to 39. Luggage racks, air brakes and air-operated doors were standard. The first RF went into service on 704 about November 1951, and the last could still be seen on Green Line duties on 725 in 1979—a remarkable span. The majority were sold for further service, many after a spell of bus work. It says much for the design that in 1965 150 RFs were given a complete re-fit and re-styling for further coach duties. These were re-classified 2RF2/4, 2RF2/5 or 2RF2/6 depending on interior equipment. The resulting external appearance, with twin headlamps and broad light green waistband contrasting with the dark green lower panels and roof, was widely acclaimed.

RF 289-294 (Total 6):
Converted from Central Area (red) buses in 1956 to boost the coach fleet. Originally 41-seaters, they were

Top: Private hire RF2 in second livery (Lens of Sutton), Left: RFW15 shows the unusual lines of the class (Lens of Sutton).

downseated to 40 on overhaul and luggage racks were fitted. (class 2RF2/3).

RF 295-313 (Total 19):
Converted from Country Area buses and seating reduced from 41 to 40 as RF 289-94. (class 2RF2/3). Originally numbered RF 514-6/697/518-32.

RF 1-25 (Total 25):
RF 1-25, classified 1RF1/2, were private hire vehicles on a 27ft. 6in. chassis with glass panels in the roof for better visibility. Resembling Green Line vehicles in their appointments, they were originally painted distinctively in green and grey, with red lettering and lining-out. Later, 10 of them, (16-25), were fitted with side brackets for destination boards, reclassified 1RF1/3 and used on Green Line duties, mainly as relief or spare vehicles. The remainder appeared in an all over green livery with red window surrounds and lettering.

RFW 1-15 (Total 15):
Specially constructed for private party and excursion work, these coaches were mechanically similar to the RF coach, except that the overall width was 8 ft. The bodywork by Eastern Coachworks seated 39 in considerable comfort, and was to a striking design, making extensive use of glass to improve visibility. They were classified 3RF3 and carried a distinctive green and grey livery and the London Transport fleetname and lining was red.

Light-weight Trials:
In 1953 three new designs of light-weight single-deckers were hired to find out whether they saved fuel and would stand up to arduous operational duties. All were lighter than the standard RF by between one and two tons. All worked for a period on 711 from Reigate Garage. They were:-
(i) A.E.C. Monocoach, chassisless, weighing 5 tons 11 cwt. (NLP 635).
(ii) Bristol LS 5G seating 45 with 5-cyl. engine, weighing 6 tons 11 cwt. (PHW 918).
(iii) Leyland Tiger Cub, with 44-seat body and weight of 5 tons 16 cwt. (PTE 592).
None carried a fleet number.

RMC4 (CRL4) (Total 1):
Heavy traffic on certain Green Line routes again

raised the issue of conversion to double-deck operation. A prototype coach, CRL 4, following closely the lines of the three RM type (Routemaster) buses then being tested in Central London, entered service in October 1957. CRL 4 embodied Leyland mechanical units and a body by Eastern Coachworks and was classified 4RM4. There were a number of important differences from the bus RM, aimed at giving the longer-distance passenger a more luxurious ride. Seating was more widely spaced, with the rear seats on the lower deck taking the form of individual bucket seats set at an angle of 45° to the front, thus reducing capacity to 55 persons. These seats were soon replaced by conventional longitudinal seats increasing the overall capacity to 57. Air suspension was employed at the rear, front suspension being by torsion bar. The electrically operated rear platform doors had open and close buttons under the control of the driver. Overhead luggage racks were provided in both saloons. The finish externally was Lincoln green with light green round the windows, although a lighter green experimental livery was carried for some time.

Experience with CRL 4 led to an order for 68

The experimental trio – top, left: Leyland Tiger Cub PTE592 (C. Carter) top, right: A.E.C. Monocoach NLP635 on bus service (Lens of Sutton), right: Bristol LS5G PHW918 (Lens of Sutton).

Routemaster coaches (RMC 1453-1520) of generally similar design and the prototype was reclassified RMC4. Later it underwent some modifications to bring it more into line with the RMC class, but was never fitted with power-assisted steering as were the rest of the RMCs. Although the front end was modified to the twin-paired headlamp design of the RMCs, the destination box and indicators remained of the three-aperture design originally fitted. It was finally withdrawn from bus service in 1979 for use in connection with the 1980 Jubilee celebrations.

RMC 1453-1520 (Total 68):
The production run of 68 Routemaster coaches differed from the prototype CRL 4 in many respects. The mechanical units were by A.E.C. and the bodies by Park Royal (class 6RM6). The frontal treatment was similar to that of the standard bus Routemaster, except for the twin-paired headlamps and the neat two-window design adopted for the service number, destination and route points display. Rear axle ratio at 4.7 to 1 was higher than that of the RM to allow for greater maximum speed. Introduced in 1962 for service on routes 715, 715A, 716, 716A, 718, 719, 720 and 720A, the RMCs had a run of seven years on a number of coach services before being relegated to Country Bus service; even by 1978/79 they were not finished, the majority being sold back to London Transport for use on driver instruction.

RCL 2218-2260 (Total 43):
This was the longer version of the Routemaster coach introduced in 1965 to give 65 seats on a 30 ft. body. Routes 715A, 721, 722, 723 and 723A were the first to receive them. The semi-automatic gearbox of the RMCs was retained, but an 11.3 litre A.E.C. engine was fitted and they were classified 8RM10. The bodies were once again by Park Royal, and were the first to carry a revised livery which included a large 'Green Line' bulls-eye transfer on the upper deck side panels under the leading window, and a new 'Green Line' fleet name on the lower side panels which did not include the words 'London Transport'. With the elimination of crew operation in the early seventies, the RCLs (apart from four retained at Godstone for rush hour workings on 709) found new duties on bus routes. All were withdrawn and sold back to London Transport during 1978/79.

Top: Prototype Routemaster coach CRL4 at Finchley (D. W. K. Jones). Right: Production RMC1474 at Aldgate (Capital Transport).

Top: Rear view of RCL2233 when new (B. E. Speller). Left: the first RC in the original experimental silver grey and green livery in 1965 (Capital Transport).

RC 1-14 (Total 14):
These fourteen coaches were high-capacity single-deckers, considerably more powerful than the RF. Introduced on 705 (Sevenoaks—Windsor) in November 1965, they were A.E.C. Reliances with an 11.3 litre engine and a 49-seat body by Willowbrook, 36 ft. long and 8 ft. 2½ in. wide, classified 1RC1. Panoramic windows, high backed seats, air suspension and forced-air ventilation made for passenger comfort. A new livery of silver and grey with a Lincoln green waistband was adopted, but later the series received standard livery. The class was dogged by mechanical unreliability and had several spells of idleness between service on 711, 723 and the Airport service 727, (for which luggage space was provided behind the driver, reducing the seating capacity to 43). After a spell on bus work the survivors were withdrawn by 1978, except for a few retained for training purposes which were disposed of in 1979.

RP 1-90 (Total 90):
The RP class were ordered to replace most of the double-deck Routemasters in Green Line service and were the first new coaches delivered to London Country. Based on the A.E.C. Reliance 6U2R chassis, they had 45-seat all-metal bodies by Park Royal, and maintained many of the improvements introduced on the RC type. The first 30 as built had rear luggage boots and all had internal parcels racks which incorporated air vents under passenger control individually. RP 1 was delivered in late 1971 and all the class had entered service by Summer 1972. Livery when new was the standard Lincoln green with a pale green band, but this was replaced by the National Bus Company green and white dual-purpose scheme on repaint in 1973/74. About half the class were refurbished in 1978/79, 30 in a modified dual-purpose livery, the others in bus livery. They are being relegated to bus and contract work as new coaches arrive. Several were sold for scrap in 1979 having been cannibalised for spares. The future of the other unrefurbished coaches, which are currently stored, is uncertain.

SMA 1-21 (Total 21):
This series of A.E.C. Swift coaches entered service in the Spring of 1972. Their 36 ft. long 45-seat Alexander bodies with wide observation windows and ramped floors were radically different in appearance

from the London Transport 'house-style' which had prevailed prior to the formation of London Country Bus Services Ltd., in 1970. Originally ordered by South Wales Transport, the SMAs were diverted to London Country and were fitted out for Green Line duties in the course of construction. The A.E.C. 8.2 litre engine was mounted horizontally at the rear under the floor. An exhaust brake was fitted. The class introduced the use of Tilling green in place of Lincoln green as the main colour. Like the RP class, they received N.B.C. dual-purpose livery on repaint. Most were withdrawn in 1978 but 4 remained in use on bus and contract work at the end of 1979.

LNC 24-70 (Total 47):
These vehicles were virtually standard Leyland National 11.3 metre long buses fitted with 49 plastic covered seats. They were the first vehicles in the new N.B.C. standard dual-purpose green and white livery. Powered by the Leyland 510 turbocharged engine, they were used on routes 721, 706 and 711 for some months before transfer to bus work.

SNC 71-97, 99-102, 104-112 (Total 40):
The next batch of Leyland National "coaches" were to the shorter 10.3 metre overall length, but were otherwise similar to the LNC's. They had their bus seats trimmed in moquette in an attempt to improve comfort. All were transferred to bus work after a short time.

SNC 116-202 (Total 87):
The final examples of Leyland National Green Line vehicles were to the new "suburban coach" specification with 39 coach type seats, overhead luggage racks and greater comfort. All will have been re-allocated to bus work when the RS/RB deliveries are completed.

RS 1-15, 31-45, 106-120, 136-150 (Total 60):
RB 16-30, 46-105, 121-135 (Total 90):
These 150 new coaches are rented on a five year term via the dealer Kirkby Central Ltd. They were delivered between 1977 and 1980. The chassis are A.E.C. Reliance fitted with the large AH 760 engine. The RS type have Plaxton bodywork built to two different styles of the "Supreme" design. The RB type have Duple Dominant II bodies. The specification of all is to the full luxury standard used

Top, left to right: RP57 at Sevenoaks (Lens of Sutton), the sorrowful front of SMA17 at Croydon (Lens of Sutton), SNC127 a "suburban coach" Leyland National (G. Brigden). Bottom, left to rigth: One of the most effective advertisers liveries was carried by RP7 (B. E. Speller), LN26 leaves Brentwood on Route 721 (G. Brigden), RS13 starts the descent of Reigate Hill (G. Brigden).

GREEN LINE
725 WINDSOR
SMA 17
JPF 117K

701 GRAVESEND
DARTFORD
GREEN LINE
PAY AS YOU ENTER PLEASE
XPD 227N

721 LONDON Aldgate
GREEN LINE
GREEN LINE
PAY AS YOU ENTER PLEASE
NPD 126L

GREEN LINE
PPH 443R

727
HEATHROW AIRPORT
GREEN LINE
GREEN LINE
PAY AS YO
ENTER PLE
PPH 446R

on coaches throughout the country and has brought new quality to the service. All seat 49 passengers and have the new standard white livery with a broad green band and large fleetname over the rear wheels. Five RBs carry the special yellow, green and white livery for Jetlink 747 and are allocated to Staines Garage. Three RBs and two RSs carry a special golden jubilee livery and will run on most services during 1980.

On Order:
2 Volvo B58, 2 Leyland Leopard:
With the cessation of production of the A.E.C. Reliance chassis a decision has to be taken on future vehicle orders. Four coaches have been ordered for delivery in early 1980 for extensive trials.

Private Hire Coaches
P 1-12, D 13-17 (Total 17):
17 A.E.C. Reliance coaches are used exclusively on express, excursion and private hire operations. They comprise five with Plaxton 49 seat bodies bought new in 1973, two with 41 seat Plaxton bodies acquired from National Travel (South-East) in 1976, five 44 or 49 seat Plaxtons from the same source in 1978 and five with Duple bodies seating 44, 49 or 51 from National Travel (London) in 1979. Two of the last batch were originally new to East Kent. The second-hand acquisitions were built in 1970-1973.

Opposite: RB16 poses for the official Duple photographer in Blackpool. Top: Jetlink 747 RB68 with Brannif jumbo jet at Gatwick (L.C.B.S.). Left: D15 en-route for East Anglia from Catford (J. G. S. Smith).

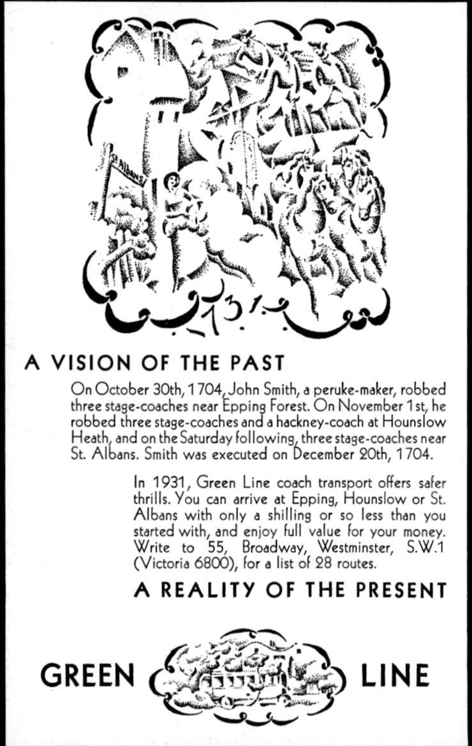

From time to time press advertising has been used to give information on Green Line services. This attractive example dates from the early 1930's.

Tickets

Did they all get on? The conductor was busy on this journey from Victoria (L.T.E.).

No story of Green Line would be complete without a chapter on the many types of tickets used over the years.

As they were intended to meet the needs of the longer distance traveller, from the early days Green Line coaches had a minimum fare in the London area of 1/- single (i.e. 12 times the bus minimum), and progressing in 3d or 6d jumps. Return tickets were available, without any time restriction, at one and a half times the single fare, rounded up to the nearest 3d as necessary. Early return issues seem to have been valid for return indefinitely, but under the control of London Transport this open-ended validity was reduced to one month. In country districts, certain fares of 9d, 6d and even 3d were provided. From 1934 onwards more of these fares were introduced together with bus fares with 1d stages on certain sections of some routes where parallel bus services had been reduced or withdrawn.

Another feature of Green Line's early days was that fare stages tended to be wide-spaced. London Transport rationalised the fare structure and introduced additional fare stages. For example, in 1930, the London to Guildford route contained seven fare stages, but by 1946 this had been increased to 21. The East London routes generally had lower fares, due to the intensive competition and the shorter distances involved. Prior to 4 October 1933 through booking facilities enabled passengers to change at Camden Town, Golders Green, Hammersmith or Shepherds Bush, and continue the journey to or from Central London by Underground. This considerably influenced ticket design.

Most Green Line tickets were of the punch variety, printed by the Bell Punch Company with a different colour for each fare value. The first appeared with the "Green Line Coaches Ltd." title and were the same style as those previously issued on the L.G.O.C. Coaches. Single tickets without Underground through booking were of the "fareboard" type (see figure 1), like L.G.O.C. bus tickets. The fareboard system enabled one to read across the ticket, to find the extent of the journey allowed for the particular fare; the conductor merely punched the stage boarded. This system needed a separate ticket-printing block for each fare value on each route, and not surprisingly was abandoned as a war-time economy measure. The equivalent return tickets (2) consisted of two sections; the top one for forward journeys, and the lower one, duplicating the stages, for the return. On issue the conductor punched the ticket in the stage boarded. On return the complete ticket would be punched in the appropriate stage and the forward portion collected to account for the punching.

For journeys to London which gave the option of Underground interchange the single tickets were printed horizontally, and specified a point-to-point booking (3) while return tickets were in two parts (4), one for each direction.

A third type of fareboard ticket was introduced in 1930 on which the title was below the serial number and the stages were pushed out to the margins with the conditions up the centre. The singles (5) showed the Underground through booking stage at the top right hand side of the ticket. After the coach had passed the interchange station if a passenger had not used the option of completing the journey by rail, the conductor would cancel the ticket with special hand nippers. Returns with Underground through bookings were in three sections with the serial number and value repeated on each (6). The first section was for the forward rail journey, the second for the coach forward journey and the third for the return journey. On the forward journey the ticket would be punched in the stage boarded, and the Underground section cancelled if necessary. When the complete ticket was presented for the return journey the conductor would retain the forward journey section, punch the return coupon in the stage boarded and issue a white exchange ticket (7) punched in the stage to which the passenger was entitled to travel. At this time tickets not containing rail through booking sections were also revised in layout to show conditions in the centre. After the introduction of through running across London higher value tickets were brought into use, but for the longest journeys two tickets would have to be issued in combination.

From 8 February 1932 Underground through booking tickets were modified to contain a separate coupon for the rail journey, thus singles became two coupon tickets while returns had four coupons (8 and 9). Value overprints were discontinued but all return tickets were overprinted "THESE TWO SECTIONS MUST BE RETAINED INTACT FOR RETURN JOURNEY". The issuing procedure was basically unaltered, the Underground section being cancelled after the coach had left the interchange point. The red "EXCHANGE" overprint was removed from exchange tickets at about this time (10). With the exception of the Watford—Golders Green and the Whipsnade routes, Underground through bookings were discontinued from 4 October 1933. As Green Line acquired various independent operators, some tickets appeared titled 'Associated', 'Blue Belle', 'Regent' and 'Skylark', whilst in the early part of 1933, the legend "Green Line Coaches and Associated Companies" appeared on some tickets. A few tickets reprinted after 1 July 1933 bore the revised title of 'London Passenger Transport Board' (11).

In those early days booking agents sold tickets but this appeared to offer little advantage, as seats were not reserved. The conductor simply treated an agent's voucher as cash, and issued a ticket in the normal way. At certain central London Underground stations it was possible to book combined Underground and coach journeys. Edmonson card tickets were issued; the singles in two portions, with the right hand one being surrendered at the interchange point and the other cancelled on the coach. The three portion return tickets were the same as singles for the forward journey, with the third section for the return journey, either by coach throughout or coach and Underground.

The 4 October 1933 re-organisation necessitated completely new ticket stocks. These were still of the fareboard type, but were not arranged for individual routes or a pair of routes as hitherto, but had all the stages for the routes operating from a particular garage or group of garages, necessitating longer tickets. The fare overprint in a circle on single tickets was somewhat unusual (12). Return tickets (13) were in two parts, with the lower section for the return journey bearing overprint 'R'. A new range of exchange tickets was issued, while a new feature was the introduction of 3d and 6d tickets for excess fares. Return tickets reprinted from 15 October 1934 had the 'R' overprint replaced by a cross and stated that they were 'available one month from date of issue'. There was, however, no reference on the ticket to the date of issue!

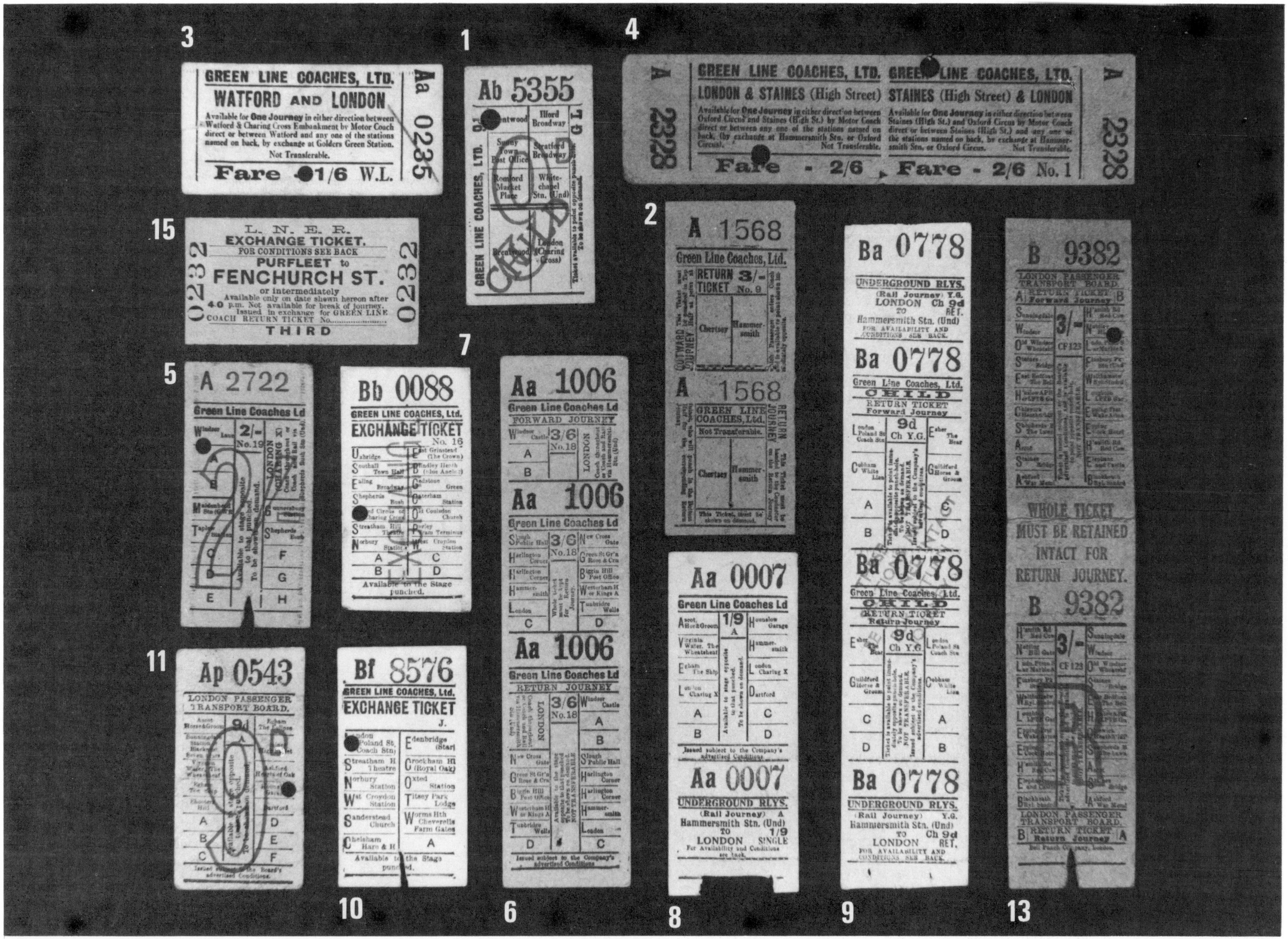
3
GREEN LINE COACHES, LTD.
WATFORD AND LONDON
Aa 0235
Not Transferable.
Fare 1/6 W.L.
1
Ab 5355
GREEN LINE COACHES, LTD.
4
GREEN LINE COACHES, LTD.
LONDON & STAINES (High Street)
STAINES (High Street) & LONDON
A 2328
Not Transferable.
Fare - 2/6
Fare - 2/6 No. 1
15
L. N. E. R.
EXCHANGE TICKET.
FOR CONDITIONS SEE BACK
PURFLEET to
FENCHURCH ST.
or intermediately
0232
THIRD
2
A 1568
Green Line Coaches, Ltd.
RETURN 3/-
TICKET No. 9
Chertsey
Hammersmith
GREEN LINE COACHES, Ltd.
Not Transferable.
5
A 2722
Green Line Coaches Ltd
7
Bb 0088
GREEN LINE COACHES, Ltd.
EXCHANGE TICKET
No. 16
Available to the Stage punched.
6
Aa 1006
Green Line Coaches Ltd
FORWARD JOURNEY
3/6
No. 18
RETURN JOURNEY
Issued subject to the Company's advertised Conditions
8
Aa 0007
Green Line Coaches Ltd
1/9
UNDERGROUND RLYS.
(Rail Journey)
Hammersmith Stn. (Und)
TO
LONDON
SINGLE
9
Ba 0778
UNDERGROUND RLYS.
(Rail Journey)
LONDON
Hammersmith Sta. (Und)
Green Line Coaches, Ltd.
CHILD
RETURN TICKET
Forward Journey
9d
Return Journey
13
B 9382
LONDON PASSENGER TRANSPORT BOARD.
Forward Journey
3/-
WHOLE TICKET MUST BE RETAINED INTACT FOR RETURN JOURNEY.
Return Journey
11
Ap 0543
LONDON PASSENGER TRANSPORT BOARD.
9d
10
Bf 8576
GREEN LINE COACHES, Ltd.
EXCHANGE TICKET
J.

From June 1935 a new type of return ticket came into use as old stocks became exhausted (14). The top section which bore the value overprint and the word 'RETURN', contained the fare stages in the centre with the conditions in the margins. These tickets were given the somewhat lengthy title 'London Passenger Transport Board (Green Line Coaches)'. The lower section was simply a perforated stub. They were issued in the normal way but on the return journey the stage at which the passenger boarded was punched (i.e. the one opposite the original punch-hole), and the stub retained (to account for the additional punching), and an exchange ticket issued. From 3 August 1935 passengers holding coach tickets from London could return by 3rd class railway without extra charge on Saturdays and Sundays after 4.00 p.m. The intact return ticket had to be presented to the railway booking clerk, who would issue a special Green Line exchange rail ticket (15).

Another new design of single and return tickets came into use on 2 May 1937. The singles (16) had the stages inset to the centre and conditions placed in the margins, while the normal 3d and 6d values incorporated an excess fare section, replacing the separate tickets. The returns were one-piece with the fare value and the word 'RETURN' overprinted, and had month and date of issue sections on both sides. The issuing conductor would clip the stage boarded with hand nippers, then punch the month and day on the front or reverse according to where the required booking appeared. On the return journey the date was indicated by clipping out all the figures *except* the relevant one in one line of the return date grid. The hour of return was also clipped with the arrow head nippers, with the arrow pointing left to indicate a.m. and right for p.m. Exchange tickets were no longer issued. Overprints were subsequently revised to delete the circle on singles and replacing "return" with the letter "R" (17). The fares revision of 27 August 1939 saw the date section on return tickets on the front only, while all tickets were titled 'London Transport (Coaches)'. (18 and 19).

Where 1d bus fare sections were included on some routes, country bus numbered stage tickets were issued for fares below 1/- other than 3d, 6d and 9d. Route B also had 1/- and 9d returns using country bus return tickets.

When Hillman's Saloon Coaches Ltd. were taken over in 1934 more than 150 insert-Setright ticket machines were acquired. This system involved the insertion of a printed ticket into the machine which printed the fare, date, stage boarded and class (20). Separate single and return tickets were provided, but as the machines could only register in 3d units, 1d and 2d excess tickets were used to make up any value. The machines were used exclusively on all coaches operating on the East London services from Romford and Grays garages until their withdrawal when the services ceased at the end of August 1939.

The "Willebrew" ticket system was the subject of experiments on the M group of routes during 1934, but as the system was not developed it must be assumed that the experiments were not successful.

The August 1939 type tickets were used as services were re-instated from late 1939, but when, from 3 July 1940, fares were increased by 10%, they continued to be issued with a second ticket, e.g. the pre-war fare of 1/6 increased to 1/9 and the 1/6 ticket would be supplemented with a 3d ticket, punched in the serial number (18). The same applied initially when the fares were further increased to 16⅔% above pre-war from 1 December 1940, but new tickets were introduced from 7 April 1941. The singles were simply country bus issues which had been retitled "London Transport (Country Buses & Coaches)" (21), while the returns were similar to the previous issues but contained a list of geographical stages and were identified by the route numbers (22). These tickets remained in use until the coaches were withdrawn in September 1942.

Season tickets were available from Green Line's earliest days but were issued only where the traffic justified it. Weekly, monthly and quarterly tickets were produced in an unusual oval shape (31). Six different colours were used with a particular colour for each week; monthly tickets had one stripe, while quarterlies bore three stripes. Unlike ordinary tickets, seasons were not valid on the Underground, except weeklies issued on the Watford services, which were produced in book form with a forward and return journey coupon for each day (32). After 14 September 1931 the books gave way to rectangular six-day tickets, from which a section was cancelled for each journey. At the same time the quarterly or monthly issues were changed to a rectangular design, the latter containing seven horizontal stripes (33). Rectangular weekly tickets, without daily cancellation sections, began to appear on other than the Watford routes from June 1932. When through running commenced season tickets were not issued for journeys across London, a restriction that was not removed until 1952. Little more is recorded about season tickets except that monthly issues appear to have been withdrawn early in 1933.

From 18 November 1934 weekly (from conductors) and four-weekly tickets (from offices) became generally available. The weekly tickets showed all fare stages on the routes of a particular garage. On issue, the stages between which the ticket was available and the date of expiry were clipped. An additional clipping indicated issue to a female passenger. The tickets catered for specific expiry dates over a three month period, requiring frequent reprinting, until 1937, when the range of expiry dates was expanded to a year (34).

New tickets were introduced from 29 December 1940 which showed stages only for the more popular journeys (35), other bookings being hand-written on blanks. The four-weekly tickets were similar to a railway season, bearing a stamped date of expiry. The issue of four-weekly tickets appears to have ceased during the early part of the war.

The Workmen's weekly tickets issued by independent operators on the Grays route were continued by London Transport. They were similar to ordinary weeklies but were restricted to one return journey each day (the outward journey to be completed before 8.00 a.m.), necessitating a clipping for each journey made (36). It was not until 1940 that these tickets were brought into line with ordinary weeklies in having a range of expiry dates for the whole year and from 29 December 1940 a design similar to the ordinary weekly tickets was issued (37).

When the Green Line network was re-instated in 1946 only single tickets were issued with the exception of routes 716 and 721, which had odd return bookings, using war-time tickets. A new series of geographical stage single tickets were produced (23), each garage or pair of garages having a set for the routes operated. Fare revisions were quite frequent in the post-war

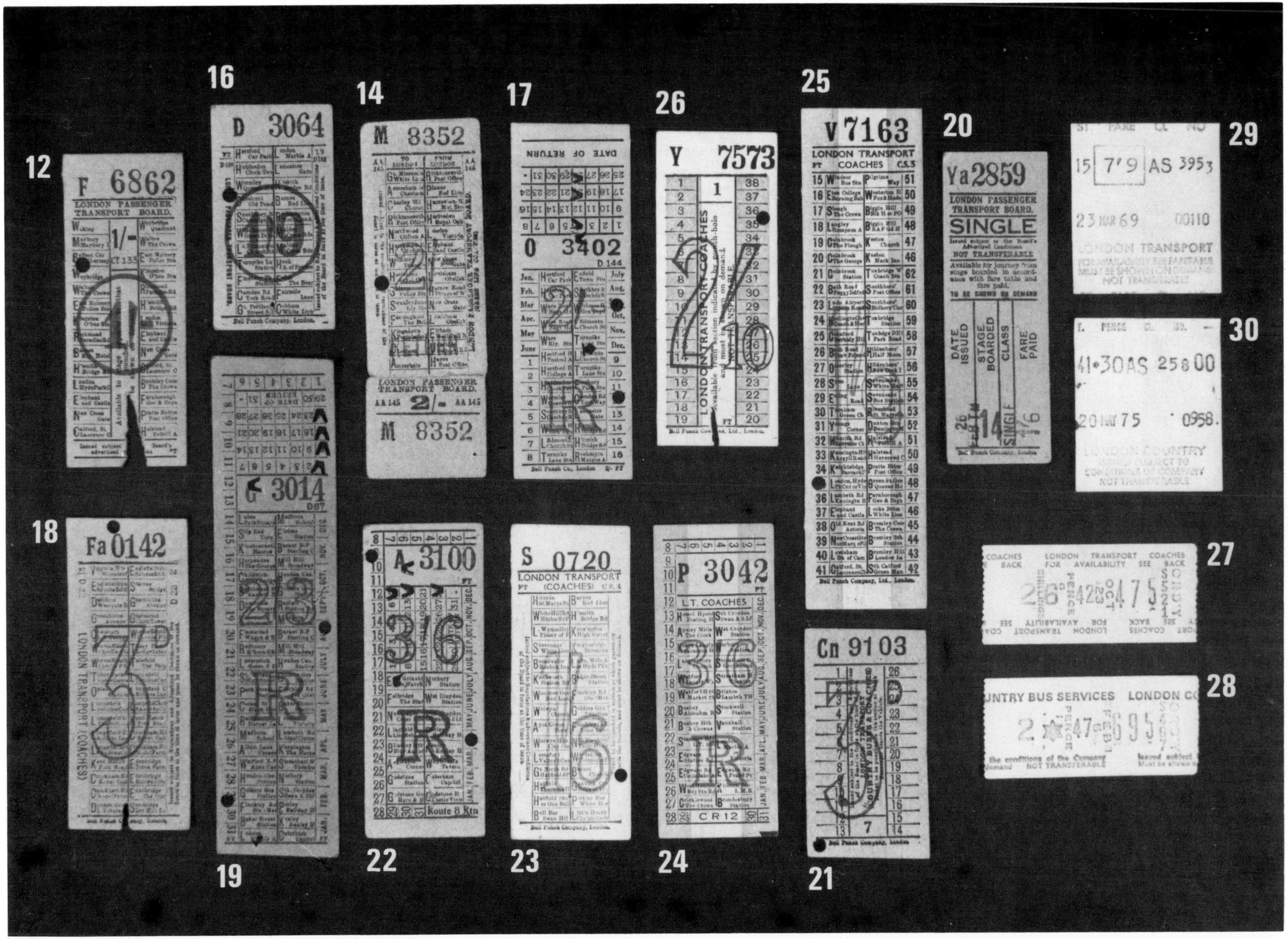
12
16
14
17
26
25
20
29
30
18
19
22
23
24
21
27
28

period and many different values were required, resulting in a colourful range of tickets. Bus fares did not apply on any routes at this period, but the one or two local fares that existed in the country area were met with the issue of low value coach tickets. The pre-war practice of issuing country bus tickets for certain short journeys was not resumed.

Six-day weekly tickets of the geographical stage type, available from Monday to Saturday, were introduced on 30 September 1946. The tickets, which were issued on the coaches, were originally yellow in colour, but from 1 October 1947 when the weekly rate was adjusted to equal nine times the single fare, the colour was changed to pink (38). Numerical stage weeklies (39) first appeared at the 1 October 1950 fares revision as a temporary substitution for the geographical issues which had not been printed in sufficient time and became general with the 2 March 1952 fares revision, except routes 721, 722 and 723/A, on which geographical tickets remained until stocks were exhausted. One such issue survived into the Autumn of 1953. Very restricted returns were introduced from 1 October 1946 to and from London on Tuesday, Wednesday and Thursday off-peaks only. The tickets were similar to the wartime numbered route issues (24). From 4 June 1948 returns were also issued on Mondays and Fridays and from 11 June 1949 they were available on Saturdays and Sundays without time restrictions. The pre-war option of returning towards London by rail after 4.00 p.m. on Saturdays and Sundays was also re-instated.

From 1 October 1950 the British Transport Commission's fares policy caused Green Line coach fares to be reduced, but return facilities, except certain bookings on routes 716, 717 and 721, were withdrawn.

The design of single tickets remained reasonably static, but from 1 January 1948 the word 'Coaches' in the title no longer appeared in brackets, and subsequently, to aid conductors, each fare stage was printed with a thick initial letter. As a prelude to mechanisation fare stage numbers were introduced on tickets from the 2 March 1952 fares revision at the same time as a number of extra fare stages were introduced requiring new single tickets (25). Central London was always stage 35. From the Spring of 1953 universal tickets, bearing stage numbers only (26), began to appear and replaced the geographical tickets from the 16 August 1953 fares revision. Route 726, however, continued to use geographical tickets without stage numbers until conversion to Setright machines.

The conversion to Setright Speed machines started with Romford Garage in May 1954 and was completed when Reigate garage was converted in January 1955. The occasional use of punch tickets continued on duplicate coaches until 1956. The Setright Speed machines issued green tickets with the title and conditions printed initially in black and subsequently in red (27). Almex ticket machines were used experimentally during 1967 on the, then, only one-man operated routes, 724 and 727 and generally with the conversion of all single-deck routes to OMO during the Winter of 1968/9 (29).

After the formation of L.C.B.S., revised Setright and Almex tickets (28 and 30) were eventually issued.The remaining crew-operated routes, except route 709, were converted to OMO in 1972, and more Almex machines were introduced. All machines in use at decimalisation in 1972 were modified to account for the new currency. Later Almex machines were capable of issuing tickets up to £9.99.

Weekly tickets underwent little change although from 1 November 1965 yellow five-day tickets were issued over sections of routes that had lost their Saturday services. London Transport-titled five and six day tickets survived decimalisation in February 1971, but certain issues were superseded by the introduction of decimal fare value tickets titled 'Green Line Weekly Ticket' before all tickets of this type were withdrawn from 3 June 1973. From this date new weekly and monthly season tickets were introduced, valid for any number of journeys. Weekly tickets were of blue print on cream card, while monthly issues were of blue print on green card. Weekly tickets were not issued on one-man-operated coaches, except by prior arrangement which involved the tickets actually being made out in advance at the garage.

With the introduction of route 727 on 13 May 1967 rail travellers via Luton and Watford Junction stations could through book to or from Heathrow Airport and continue their journey on the coach. A range of Edmonson card rail tickets was provided. This facility was later extended to include Gatwick to Heathrow bookings.

On 16 August 1970 Golden Rover tickets were introduced, as an extension of the well-established Green Rover facility, to cover both bus services and Green Line Coaches, except initially route 727. The tickets issued on the coaches were from either the Setright or Almex machines, but pre-printed tickets were provided for issue on certain 'Autofare' bus routes until 1972.

Jetlink 747 service uses paper tickets in pads, yellow for on-coach issues and green for agents. Only £2.50 singles are offered.

During the Summer of 1979 combined tickets were issued from Victoria to Windsor allowing entry to the Safari Park or a ride on the Windsorian open-top bus tour.

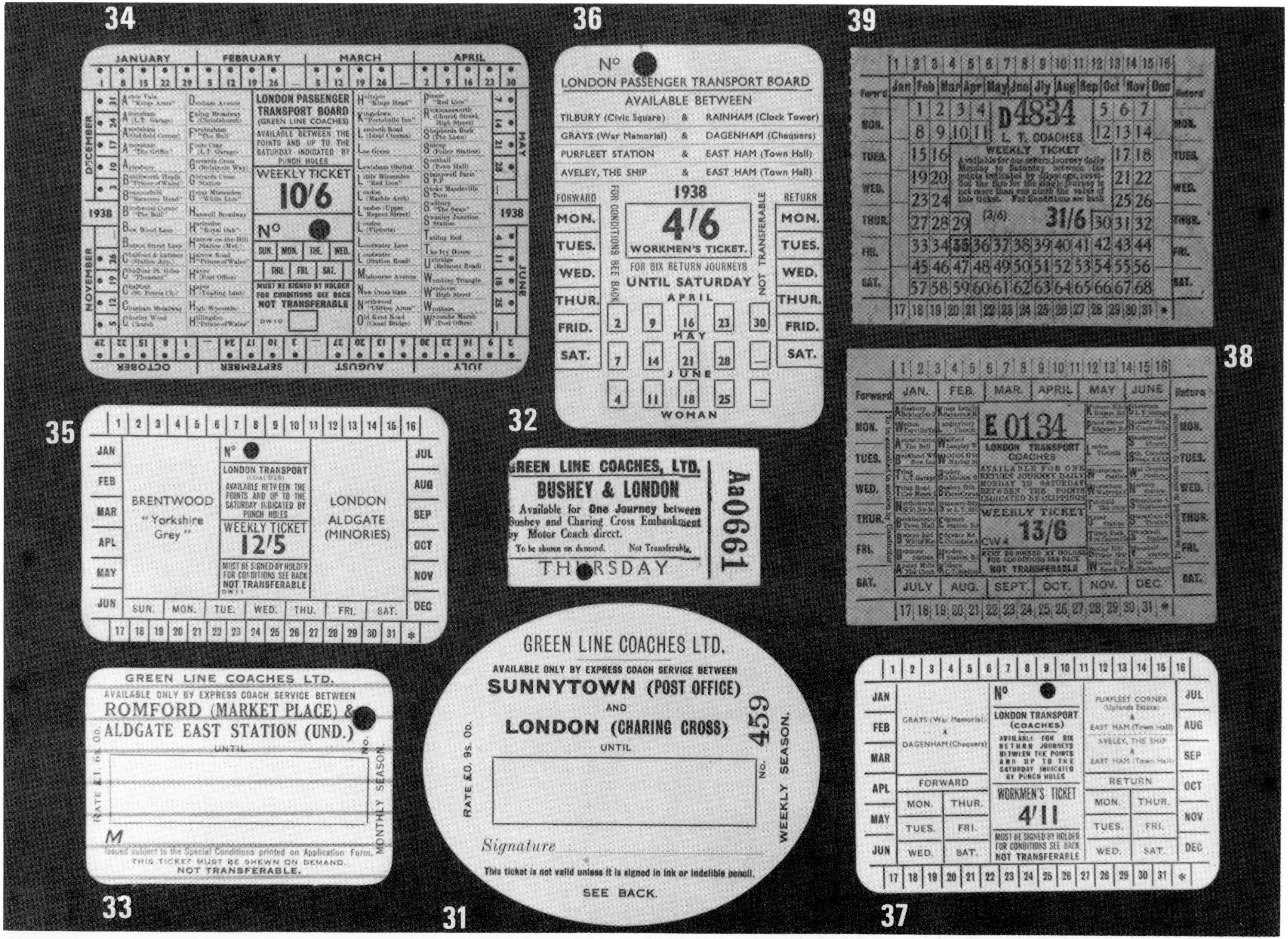
34
LONDON PASSENGER TRANSPORT BOARD
(GREEN LINE COACHES)
AVAILABLE BETWEEN THE POINTS AND UP TO THE SATURDAY INDICATED BY PUNCH HOLES
WEEKLY TICKET
10/6
MUST BE SIGNED BY HOLDER FOR CONDITIONS SEE BACK NOT TRANSFERABLE
36
LONDON PASSENGER TRANSPORT BOARD
AVAILABLE BETWEEN
TILBURY (Civic Square) & RAINHAM (Clock Tower)
GRAYS (War Memorial) & DAGENHAM (Chequers)
PURFLEET STATION & EAST HAM (Town Hall)
AVELEY, THE SHIP & EAST HAM (Town Hall)
1938
4/6
WORKMEN'S TICKET.
FOR SIX RETURN JOURNEYS
UNTIL SATURDAY
WOMAN
39
D4834
L. T. COACHES
WEEKLY TICKET
31/6
38
E 0134
LONDON TRANSPORT COACHES
AVAILABLE FOR ONE RETURN JOURNEY DAILY MONDAY TO SATURDAY BETWEEN THE POINTS INDICATED BY CLIPPINGS
WEEKLY TICKET
13/6
35
BRENTWOOD "Yorkshire Grey"
LONDON ALDGATE (MINORIES)
LONDON TRANSPORT (COACHES)
WEEKLY TICKET
12/5
32
GREEN LINE COACHES, LTD.
BUSHEY & LONDON
Available for One Journey between Bushey and Charing Cross Embankment by Motor Coach direct.
To be shown on demand. Not Transferable.
THURSDAY
Aa0661
33
GREEN LINE COACHES LTD.
AVAILABLE ONLY BY EXPRESS COACH SERVICE BETWEEN
ROMFORD (MARKET PLACE) & ALDGATE EAST STATION (UND.)
UNTIL
RATE £1. 6s. 0d.
MONTHLY SEASON.
Issued subject to the Special Conditions printed on Application Form.
THIS TICKET MUST BE SHEWN ON DEMAND.
NOT TRANSFERABLE.
31
GREEN LINE COACHES LTD.
AVAILABLE ONLY BY EXPRESS COACH SERVICE BETWEEN
SUNNYTOWN (POST OFFICE)
AND
LONDON (CHARING CROSS)
UNTIL
RATE £0. 9s. 0d.
No. 459
WEEKLY SEASON.
Signature
This ticket is not valid unless it is signed in ink or indelible pencil.
SEE BACK.
37
GRAYS (War Memorial) & DAGENHAM (Chequers)
LONDON TRANSPORT (COACHES)
AVAILABLE FOR SIX RETURN JOURNEYS BETWEEN THE POINTS AND UP TO THE SATURDAY INDICATED BY PUNCH HOLES
WORKMEN'S TICKET
4/11
MUST BE SIGNED BY HOLDER FOR CONDITIONS SEE BACK NOT TRANSFERABLE
PURFLEET CORNER (Uplands Estate) & EAST HAM (Town Hall)
AVELEY, THE SHIP & EAST HAM (Town Hall)

Destinations by the score are carried on the linen destination blinds in all coaches. Traditionally these were always manufactured by London Transport themselves, but are now bought from specialist suppliers.

Chronology of service changes

The familiar exterior of Reigate garage (H. J. Snook).

7 AUG 1928	East Surrey commences Redhill-Reigate-Northumberland Avenue and Reigate-Redhill-Northumberland Avenue
2 MAR 1929	Last day of operation of above services
2 OCT 1929	General commences Watford-Golders Green with through bookings to London by Underground from Golders Green
12 NOV 1929	Above service suspended
18 DEC 1929	General reinstates Watford-Golders Green and introduces a new route Watford-Stanmore-Charing Cross Underground Stn.
20 APL 1930	General commences Windsor-Slough-Colnbrook-Charing Cross
6 JUNE 1930	Autocar commences Tunbridge Wells-Oxford Circus.
	East Surrey commences Dorking-Epsom-Oxford Circus. Redhill-Croydon-Oxford Circus. Reigate-Sutton-Oxford Circus
9 JULY 1930	Green Line Coaches Ltd. of 55 Broadway, SW1 registered as a company with a capital of £20,000
10 JULY 1930	General commences Windsor-Staines-Hounslow-Charing Cross
17 JULY 1930	Green Line commences Guildford-Ripley-Kingston-by-pass-Charing Cross
	The two Watford services use newly delivered T type coaches carrying the Green Line fleet name
23 JULY 1930	Green Line commences Brentwood-Romford-Aldgate-Charing Cross
	General commences Sunningdale-Staines-Hounslow-Charing Cross
2 AUG 1930	General commences Maidenhead-Slough-Gt. West Rd.-Charing Cross
1 SEPT 1930	General commences Ascot-Staines-Hounslow-Oxford Circus
8 SEPT 1930	Green Line commences Tring-Bushey-Stanmore-Charing Cross but is not allowed to pick up or set down in Watford
17 SEPT 1930	National as operating agent for Green Line commences Welwyn Garden City-Hatfield-Brookmans Park-Charing Cross
20 SEPT 1930	Green Line commences Harpenden-St. Albans-Radlett-Mill Hill-Charing Cross
29 SEPT 1930	East Surrey commences Godstone Green-Whyteleafe-Croydon-Oxford Circus
1 OCT 1930	East Surrey commences Great Bookham-Epsom-Oxford Circus
	National as operating agent for Green Line commences Bishop's Stortford-Epping-Loughton-Finsbury Park-Charing Cross
	General Ascot, Sunningdale and Windsor via Staines routes transferred to Green Line
8 OCT 1930	East Surrey commences Westerham-Bromley-Oxford Circus
11 OCT 1930	Green Line commences Chertsey-Weybridge-Dittons-Kingston-Richmond-Charing Cross
18 OCT 1930	General Maidenhead and Windsor via Slough routes transferred to Green Line
18 OCT 1930	Westerham route is extended to Sevenoaks
22 OCT 1930	East Surrey commences Oxted-Chelsham-Croydon-Oxford Circus
1 NOV 1930	All routes leaving Charing Cross via Aldwych, Bush House are diverted via Northumberland Avenue
12 NOV 1930	East Surrey commences East Grinstead-Caterham-on-the-Hill-Croydon-Oxford Circus
	Redhill route is extended to Crawley
22 NOV 1930	National as operating agent for Green Line commences Hertford-Ware-Enfield-Charing Cross
29 NOV 1930	Ascot and Sunningdale routes are diverted via Ashford and Feltham and Ascot route is also altered to terminate at Charing Cross
6 DEC 1930	Oxted route is extended to Edenbridge
10 DEC 1930	First Green Line through routes across London: Reigate-Oxford Circus-Welwyn Garden City. Great Bookham-Oxford Circus-Harpenden
25 DEC 1930	Opening of purpose-built Poland Street Green Line Coach Station. Guildford and Windsor via Staines routes are diverted to terminate at the coach station
4 JAN 1931	Maidenhead route diverted to Poland Street Coach Station
11 JAN 1931	Ascot, Sunningdale and Chertsey routes diverted to Poland Street Coach Station.
14 JAN 1931	Dorking, Edenbridge, Hertford, Sevenoaks via Westerham and Tunbridge Wells routes diverted to Poland Street Coach Station
	East Grinstead route diverted via Whyteleafe and into Poland Street Coach Station
	Reigate-Welwyn Garden City route extended to Hitchin
	More through routes established: Crawley-Redhill-Oxford Circus extended to Bushey. Godstone Green-Caterham-on-the-Hill-Oxford Circus-Tring.
	New route Caterham-Coulsdon-Croydon-Oxford Circus-Bushey-Hemel Hempstead (but without stops in Watford)
26 JAN 1931	Amersham & District commences Amersham (Oakfield Corner)-Gerrards Cross-Oxford Circus
28 JAN 1931	East Surrey commences Farningham-Poland Street Coach Station
	Ascot, Sunningdale and Windsor via Staines routes diverted from Syon Lane and Great West Road to run via Brentford High Street. Ascot, Sunningdale routes also diverted from Poland St. and extended via Northumberland Ave. (W/B), Gt. Scotland Yard (E/B) to Dartford
31 JAN 1931	Green Line commences: Sunbury Common-Kingston-Richmond-Poland St. Coach Stn.
	West Byfleet-Kingston-by-pass-Poland St. Coach Stn.
	Rickmansworth-Harrow-Wembley-Poland St. Coach Stn.
1 FEB 1931	Amersham service extended to Chesham
7 FEB 1931	Green Line commences Uxbridge-Poland Street Coach Station
9 FEB 1931	Coach services commencing after this date could not continue to operate after 31st March 1931 unless licensed by the Traffic Commissioner
18 FEB 1931	Tring route extended to Aylesbury
21 FEB 1931	Route letters were allocated to Green Line services as follows: A Dartford-Gt. Scotland Yard-Ascot or Sunningdale B Brentwood-Charing Cross C Chertsey-Poland Street Coach Station D Dorking-Poland Street Coach Station E Crawley-Redhill-Oxford Circus-Bushey F Hertford-Poland Street Coach Station G Guildford-Poland Street Coach Station H Harpenden-Oxford Circus-Great Bookham I Farningham-Poland Street Coach Station J Edenbridge-Chelsham-Poland Street Coach Station K Caterham-Oxford Circus-Hemel Hempstead L Tunbridge Wells-Poland Street Coach Station M Maidenhead-Poland Street Coach Station N Windsor-Staines-Poland Street Coach Station O Bishop's Stortford-Charing Cross P Rickmansworth-Poland Street Coach Station Q Uxbridge-Poland Street Coach Station R Reigate-Oxford Circus-Hitchin S Sunbury Common-Poland Street Coach Station T Godstone Green-Oxford Circus-Aylesbury U East Grinstead-Poland Street Coach Station V Watford-Golders Green W Watford-Charing Cross X Sevenoaks-Westerham-Poland Street Coach Station Y West Byfleet-Poland Street Coach Station Z Windsor-Slough-Charing Cross
21 FEB 1931	New route AV Upminster, Bell-Barking-Charing Cross
1 APL 1931	Route AV withdrawn and Route T curtailed at Tring to comply with Road Traffic Act 1930.
22 OCT 1931	Amersham & District Chesham service curtailed at Amersham and prevented from stopping in the Denham area by decision of Southern Area Traffic Commissioner
6 FEB 1932	Skylark Motor Coach Co. Ltd. acquired: Hertford Heath- Oxford Circus (AF). Guildford-Oxford Circus (BG). High Wycombe-Oxford Circus (AQ)
20 FEB 1932	Bucks Expresses (Watford) Ltd. service acquired: Watford (Buck's Garage, The Parade)-Oxford Circus (AW)
2 MAR 1932	Regent Motor Service acquired: Hertford-Oxford Circus (CF)
16 MAR 1932	Route D curtailed to terminate at newly-opened Dorking Garage from its original terminal at Falkland Arms
24 MAR 1932	New route BH introduced: Baker Street Stn.-Whipsnade (Limited Stop)
29 MAR 1932	Route BH terminal changed to Marylebone Station
20 JULY 1932	Blue Belle Motors Ltd. acquired: East Grinstead-Paddington (Spring Street) (AU)
22 SEPT 1932	Acme Pullman Services Ltd. taken over by

L.G.O.C. and the route, Newmarket-Stansted-Bishop's Stortford-Charing Cross operated by Green Line under the 'ACME' name without a route letter

30 NOV 1932 Red Rover Saloon Coaches acquired: Aylesbury-Marble Arch-Seymour Street (Limited Stop), retaining through bookings to Buckingham until 13 Jan 1933

26 APL 1933 Queen Line Coaches acquired: Baldock-Kings Cross Coach Stn. (AR)

1 JULY 1933 LONDON PASSENGER TRANSPORT BOARD FORMED.
Route A extended from Dartford to Gravesend, Denton.
Route I extended from Farningham to Wrotham.
'ACME' service withdrawn between Newmarket and Bishop's Stortford.
Lewis's Cream Line Coaches acquired: Brookmans Park-Portman Square (BR).
West Herts Motor Services Ltd. acquired: Hemel Hempstead-Watford-by-pass-Marylebone (AK)

3 OCT 1933 Poland Street Coach Station closed to the public after this day and most Green Line services diverted from Central London in accordance with Amulree Committee rulings.
Maidenhead and Windsor via Slough routes (M and Z) withdrawn.

4 OCT 1933 A new pattern of Green Line routes commences with the main stopping place in London at Eccleston Bridge, Victoria and all other boarding points within the Metropolitan Traffic Area widely spaced and precisely detailed in publicity material and identified by roadside stop signs. Coaches could continue to set down anywhere en route. A route lettering scheme was introduced starting at Gravesend (A) thence in a clockwise direction, finishing with Tilbury (Z). The new network was as follows:

A Gravesend, Denton-Victoria-Ascot
AA Gravesend, Denton-Victoria-Sunningdale
B Wrotham-Victoria-Rickmansworth
C Tunbridge Wells-Victoria-Chertsey
AC Tunbridge Wells (Sats p.m. & Suns.)-Sevenoaks-Victoria-Woking
D Sevenoaks-Westerham Hill-Victoria-Sunbury Common
E Edenbridge-Chelsham-Victoria-Tring
F Tatsfield-Chelsham-Victoria-Hemel Hempstead
AF Portman Square-Hemel Hempstead
G Caterham-Horse Guards Avenue
H East Grinstead-Victoria-Harpenden
AH East Grinstead-Victoria-Dunstable
I Crawley-Redhill-Oxford Circus-Watford
J Reigate-Oxford Circus-Watford
K Dorking-Victoria-Welwyn Garden City-Hitchin
AK Kings Cross-Baldock
L Great Bookham-Victoria-Uxbridge
M Guildford-Oxford Circus-Enfield-Hertford
AM Guildford (Sats. p.m. & Suns.)-Esher-Oxford Circus-Great Cambridge Rd.-Hertford
BM Byfleet-Oxford Circus-Great Cambridge Road-Hertford
N Windsor-Portman Square-Epping
Q High Wycombe-Oxford Circus
R Amersham-Oxford Circus
AT Aylesbury-Marble Arch (Limited Stop)
T Watford-Golders Green Station
U Whipsnade Zoo-Marylebone Station (Limited Stop)
V Bishop's Stortford-Liverpool Street extended to Horse Guards Avenue M-F evenings, Sats. p.m. & Sun.
W Ongar-Liverpool Street
Y Brentwood-Romford-Aldgate extended to Horse Guards Avenue M-F evenings, Sats. p.m. & Suns.

25 OCT 1933 New route X Gidea Park-Romford-Eastern Avenue-Aldgate extended to Horse Guards Avenue Sats. p.m. & Suns.

During NOV 1933 Additional boarding points authorised on all routes

1 DEC 1933 J.H. Price (Super Coaches) service acquired: Route AZ East Ham-Aveley

20 DEC 1933 Premier Line acquired: Route O Trafalgar Square-Windsor via Colnbrook By-Pass. Route P Trafalgar Square-Farnham Common via Colnbrook Village

23 DEC 1933 Battens (Amalgamated Omnibus Services & Supplies Ltd.) service acquired: Route Z Aldgate, Mansell St.-Grays-Tilbury Dock Station

3 JAN 1934 Route D extended from Sunbury to Staines Garage

10 JAN 1934 Edward Hillman's Saloon Coaches Ltd., and its associate Upminster Services Ltd., acquired: Bow-Brentwood (absorbed into route Y). Route AY Aldgate, Mansell Street-Upminster

17 JAN 1934 West London Coaches acquired: Route S Victoria Coach Station-Rickmansworth-Amersham-Aylesbury with connecting shuttle service Amersham-Chesham

25 JAN 1934 Sunset Pullman Coaches Ltd. acquired: Aldgate-Brentwood (absorbed into route Y including Sunday afternoon journeys to Brentwood, Highwood Hospital)

1 FEB 1934 Strawhatter Motor Services acquired: Route BH Kings Cross Coach Stn.-Barnet-Luton

21 FEB 1934 Routes E & F diverted at Bushey away from Aldenham Road and Watford-By-Pass to run via Watford High Street

22 FEB 1934 Fleet Transport Services Ltd. all-night Aldgate-Romford service acquired and merged into route Y

10 MAR 1934 Route Z terminal changed to Aldgate Minories lay-by

19 APL 1934 Route AY terminal changed to Aldgate Minories lay-by

25 APL 1934 Route H diverted away from Lingfield via Eastbourne Road.
Route AH diverted between Lingfield and East Grinstead via Baldwin's Hill

27 APL 1934 Beaumont-Safeway Coaches London-Dunstable service acquired without apparent alteration to route AH

13 JUNE 1934 Route Y all-night service transferred to Central bus route 617

13 JULY 1934 Routes AF, S, AT last day of operation

14 JULY 1934 Route B extended from Rickmansworth to Amersham with alternate journeys continuing to either Aylesbury or Chesham.
Route E extended from Tring to Aylesbury but curtailed at Chelsham apart from odd journeys to Tatsfield
Route F alternate journeys extended from Chelsham to Edenbridge; the other alternate journey continued to Tatsfield
Route I extended from Watford to Abbots Langley

18 JULY 1934 Route Z aborbs route AZ and is extended in Tilbury to Feenan Highway

19 SEPT 1934 Route H extended from Harpenden to Luton, also diverted between Apex Corner and Allum Lane Corner via Watford-By-Pass and Elstree

26 SEPT 1934 Routes A and AA curtailed at Gravesend Clock Tower

8 MAY 1935 Route AY extended from Upminster to Corbets Tey

5 JUNE 1935 Route Z redesignated Z1.
New route Z2 Aldgate-Averley-Grays

26 JUNE 1935 Route Y redesignated Y1.
Route AY redesignated Y2 and certain journeys are diverted to terminate at Hornchurch Station.

3 JULY 1935 Route A redesignated A1.
Route AA redesignated A2.
Route P extended Sats. p.m. & Suns. to Burnham Beeches.

31 JULY 1935 Route C additional service operates Tunbridge Wells-Victoria following acquisition from Maidstone and District of former Redcar service

14 AUG 1935 Route BM diverted between Hoddesdon and Hertford to run via Hertford Heath

7 SEPT 1935 Route N alternate journeys extended on Sats. p.m. & Suns. from Epping to Bishop's Stortford

8 JAN 1936 Route B Chesham journeys diverted at Amersham to continue on main route to Wendover
Route C redesignated C1.
Route AC redesignated C2 and revised to run daily Tunbridge Wells-Victoria-Woking thus integrating former Redcar service
Route H redesignated H1, diverted to serve Lingfield; also diverted away from Elstree Village to serve Borehamwood and Barnet By-Pass
Route AH redesignated H2
Route K redesignated K1 and extended from Hitchin to Baldock to replace withdrawn route

AK. Alternate journeys to Welwyn Garden City terminate at Longcroft Green instead of Cherry Tree
New route K2 covering part of route AK and stage section of former Fairways Coaches (Kings Cross-Worthing service). Horsham-Dorking-Kingston-Victoria-Barnet-By-Pass-Welwyn Gdn. City Stn. extended Sats. p.m. & Suns. to Hitchin.
Routes M, AM and BM redesignated M1, M3 and M2 respectively
Route R extended from Amersham to Chesham
Route T redesignated T1.
New route T2 Watford-Golders Green Stn. via Elstree Village and Stirling Corner

5 FEB 1936 Route Z1 terminal in Tilbury changed to Civic Square

4 MAR 1936 Route D terminal in Sevenoaks changed to Bligh's Meadow Car Park (Bus Station)

30 MAY 1936 Route L Sat. p.m. and Sun. journeys extended alternately from Uxbridge to Chesham as L1 and High Wycombe as L2

29 JULY 1936 Route BH redesignated H3

2 AUG 1936 New route Y3 Sundays only Windsor-Slough-Trafalgar Square-Aldgate-Brentwood-Highwood Hospital

19 AUG 1936 Route X curtailed at Romford Market Place

30 AUG 1936 Garage journeys to work in service (with 1d fares): Route M2 Addlestone-Byfleet Corner. Route G Godstone-Caterham. Route I Reigate-Redhill via Blackborough Road

4 OCT 1936 Routes L1, L2 last day of operation

16 DEC 1936 Route P garage journeys with 1d fares, Windsor-Farnham Common introduced as Slough Bath Road garage closes and allocation is operated from Windsor

2 MAY 1937 Routes A1 and A2 diverted between Northfleet and Gravesend to run via London Road and Overcliffe
Route G extended from Horse Guards Avenue to Windsor via Slough. Also diverted between Purley and Thornton Heath via Purley Way to serve Croydon Airport
Route L withdrawn, replaced by extension of route O and an increased service on route R
Route M1 diverted between Southbury Road and Waltham Cross via Great Cambridge Road instead of routes M2 and M3 which were diverted via Ponders End
Route N seasonal extension from Epping to Bishop's Stortford commences
Route O extended from Trafalgar Square to Great Bookham replacing route L
Route P London terminal altered to Horse Guards Avenue
Route T2 withdrawn. Route T1 redesignated T.

MAY 1937 In view of the changes since October 1933 it seems appropriate to list the routes now running.

A1 Gravesend-Victoria Ascot
A2 Gravesend-Victoria-Sunningdale
B Wrotham-Victoria-Wendover-Aylesbury
C1 Tunbridge Wells-Victoria-Chertsey
C2 Tunbridge Wells-Victoria-Woking
D Sevenoaks-Westerham Hill-Victoria-Staines
E Chelsham-Victoria-Tring-Aylesbury
F Edenbridge or Tatsfield-Victoria-Hemel Hempstead
G Caterham-Trafalgar Square-Slough-Windsor
H1 East Grinstead-Victoria-Luton
H2 East Grinstead-Victoria-Dunstable
H3 Kings Cross Coach Station-Barnet-Luton
I Crawley-Redhill-Oxford Circus-Watford-Abbots Langley
J Reigate-London-Watford
K1 Dorking-Victoria-Welwyn Garden City-Baldock
K2 Horsham-Victoria-Welwyn Garden City extended to Hitchin (Sat. p.m. & Suns. p.m.)
M1 Guildford-Oxford Circus-Enfield-Ware-Hertford
M2 Byfleet-Oxford Circus-Ponders End-Hertford Heath-Hertford
M3 Guildford (Sats. p.m. & Suns.)-Esher-Oxford Circus-Ponders End-Ware-Hertford
N Windsor-Portman Square-Epping extended to Bishop's Stortford, Summer Sats. p.m. & Suns.
O Great Bookham-Leatherhead-Trafalgar Square-Slough-Windsor
P Horse Guards Ave-Farnham Common extended to Burnham Beeches Summer Sats. p.m. & Suns.
Q High Wycombe-Oxford Circus
R Chesham-Amersham-Uxbridge-Oxford Circus
T Watford-Golders Green Station
U Whipsnade Zoo-Marylebone Station
V Bishop's Stortford-Liverpool Street extended to Horse Guards Avenue MF evgs, Sats. p.m. & Suns.
W Ongar-Liverpool Street
X Romford-Eastern Avenue-Aldgate extended to Horse Guards Avenue Sats. p.m. & Suns.
Y1 Brentwood-Romford-Aldgate extended to Horse Guards Avenue MF evgs, Sats. p.m. & Suns. (Coaches run to Brentwood, Highwood Hospital Sun. Afts.)
Y2 Corbets Tey or Hornchurch Station-Aldgate
Y3 Windsor-Trafalgar Square-Brentwood extended afts. to Highwood Hospital-Summer Sundays only
Z1 Tilbury-Grays-Purfleet-Aldgate
Z2 Grays-Aveley-Aldgate

3 OCT 1937 Route P last day of Saturday operation

6 OCT 1937 Route V withdrawn between Liverpool Street and Horse Guards Avenue.
Routes X & Y1 withdrawn between Aldgate and Horse Guards Avenue

9 FEB 1938 Route D withdrawn between Sevenoaks and Westerham.
Route K1 diverted between Hatfield Stn. and Stanborough to run via The Stone House and By-Pass Road
Route K2 revised to run Dorking-Epsom-Victoria-Potters Bar-South Mimms-Welwyn Garden City
New route K3 Horsham-Dorking-Kingston-Baker Street Station
Route O withdrawn

1 SEPT 1939 Green Line Coaches withdrawn for immediate conversion to public ambulances and the routes suspended. It seems that Romford Garage operated a service for a day or two longer

25 SEPT 1939 New Country Bus routes introduced to cover the bus fare sections of withdrawn coach routes and also maintain a link to Tunbridge Wells

Route	Termini	Replacing
369	St. Albans-Dunstable	H2
371	East Ham-Aveley-Grays	Z2
371A	East Ham-By-Pass Road-Grays	Z1
380A	Broxbourne-Hertford Heath-Hertford	M2
392	Ongar-Woodford Wells	W
393	Amersham-Great Missenden	B
396	Epping-Bishop's Stortford	V
403C	Warlingham-Tatsfield	F
403D	Sevenoaks-Tunbridge Wells	C1,C2
465	Warlingham-Edenbridge	F
478	Swanley-Wrotham	B

It is probable that some journeys over at least part of these routes had been operated by un-numbered buses from soon after the coaches, withdrawal

1 NOV 1939 Routes Y1, Z1 and Z2 re-instated except for the Z1 Grays-Tilbury section

13 DEC 1939 Route Y2 re-instated

17 JAN 1940 Routes A1, A2, Q and R re-instated

7 FEB 1940 Route H1 re-instated between Luton and Victoria only
Route M1 re-instated to operate Hertford-Oxford Circus daily extended Weekdays to Shepherds Bush

13 MAR 1940 Route C1 re-instated and redesignated C
Route E re-instated between Aylesbury and Victoria only
Route F re-instated between Hemel Hempstead and Victoria only
Route H1 extended through to East Grinstead and re-designated H

8 MAY 1940 Route N re-instated between Portman Square and Epping continuing to Bishop's Stortford Sats. p.m. & Suns.

18 JUNE 1940 Route M terminates at Oxford Circus daily

23 OCT 1940 Routes A1, A2, C and H crossing London are

split into two sections, each terminating at Victoria

4 DEC 1940 A revised network of numbered routes introduced, all terminating in central London. The numbers were allotted to avoid duplication with Central Bus routes serving the same roads. The re-instated routes were as follows: (the letters in brackets being the pre-war route)

2	(A)	Gravesend-Victoria
3	(B)	Wrotham-Victoria
5	(C1)	Tunbridge Wells-Victoria
8	(H1)	East Grinstead-Victoria
9	(I)	Crawley-Redhill-Oxford Circus
10	(J)	Reigate-Oxford Circus
18	(M1)	Guildford-Oxford Circus
20	(C1)	Chertsey-Victoria
23	(A1)	Ascot-Victoria
23A	(A2)	Sunningdale-Victoria
33	(Q)	High Wycombe-Oxford Circus
34	(R)	Chesham-Amersham-Oxford Circus
35	(B)	Aylesbury-Rickmansworth-Victoria
40	(E)	Aylesbury-Tring-Victoria
40A	(F)	Hemel Hempstead-Victoria
40B	(I/J)	Watford-Leavesden Rd. Garage-Victoria*
45	(H1)	Luton-Radlett-Victoria
46	(H3)	Luton-Barnet-Victoria
49	(M1)	Hertford-Oxford Circus
52	(N)	Epping-Oxford Circus
53	(V)	Bishop's Stortford-Aldgate
55	(Y1)	Brentwood-Romford-Aldgate
58	(Y2)	Corbets Tey or Hornchurch Stn.-Aldgate§
59	(Z1)	Grays-By-Pass Road-Aldgate
59A	(Z2)	Grays-Aveley-Aldgate

* Route 40B—there is some doubt as to whether this service actually operated, if it ran at all, it was withdrawn after 17th December 1940.
§ Route 58 was originally advertised as route 56.

18 DEC 1940 Other routes re-instated were:

14	(K1)	Dorking-Epsom-Victoria
15	(K3)	Dorking-Kingston-Victoria
21	(D)	Staines-Kingston-Victoria*
26	(G)	Windsor-Slough-Victoria
26A	(P)	Farnham Common-Victoria
47	(K1)	Hitchin-Victoria
47A	(K2)	Welwyn Garden City-Victoria
54	(X)	Romford-Eastern Avenue-Aldgate

*Route 21 was originally advertised as route 25.

29 SEPT 1942 Last day of operation in wartime of Green Line coaches. In order to place restrictions on unnecessary travel and to conserve fuel and rubber all Green Line coaches were withdrawn after this date for the duration of the war.

1946 A revised Green Line network, numbered in the 700 series in a clockwise sequence from Gravesend, was introduced in the following order as crews and vehicles became available:

6 FEB 1946	715	Guildford-Oxford Circus-Hertford
	720	Bishop's Stortford-Aldgate
6 MAR 1946	704	Tunbridge-Wells-Victoria-Windsor
	709	Caterham-Baker Street Station
	710	Crawley-Baker Street Station
	721	Brentwood-Aldgate
	723	Tilbury-Grays-Aldgate
8 MAR 1946	716	Chertsey-Marble Arch-Hitchin
3 APRL 1946	703	Wrotham-Victoria-Amersham
	711	Reigate-Baker Street Station
	718	Windsor-Kingston-Victoria-Epping
	722	Corbets Tey or Hornchurch Station-Aldgate
	724	High Wycombe-Oxford Circus
1 MAY 1946	708	East Grinstead-Victoria-Hemel Hempstead
	714	Dorking-Kingston-Baker Street Station
	717	Woking-Marble Arch-Welwyn Garden City
	727	Luton-Barnet-Kings Cross Coach Station
29 MAY 1946	705	Sevenoaks-Westerham-Victoria-Windsor
	712	Dorking-Epsom-Victoria-Radlett-Luton
	713	Dorking-Epsom-Victoria-Radlett-Dunstable
	726	Marylebone Stn.-Whipsnade Zoo (Limited Stop, Summer only)
19 JUNE 1946	725	Chesham-Amersham-Oxford Circus
	702	Gravesend-Victoria-Sunningdale
22 JUNE 1946	701	Gravesend-Victoria-Ascot
26 JUNE 1946	706	Westerham-Victoria-Aylesbury
	707	Oxted-Victoria-Aylesbury

It should be noted that the number 719 does not appear in this list. This route was intended to operate between Windsor and Luton via Uxbridge, Watford and St. Albans out of which express bus 803 emerged some years later.

2 OCT 1946 Route 709 extended to work in service between Caterham and Godstone Garage

29 SEPT 1947 Route 727 diverted to terminate at a temporary coach station at Kings Cross Judd Street

11 NOV 1947 Routes 724 and 725 last day of operation

12 NOV 1947 Route 709 extended from Baker Street to Chesham via 725
Route 710 extended from Baker Street to Amersham via 725
Route 711 extended from Baker Street to High Wycombe via 724

26 MAR 1948 Route 726. London terminal changed to Baker Street, Allsop Place

19 MAY 1948 Route 708 certain journeys diverted away from Lingfield to run direct via Eastbourne Road

9 JUNE 1948 Route 706 journeys diverted to double run via Tatsfield

25 AUG 1948 Route 716 extended to Chertsey Bridge

2 MAR 1949 Route 708 all journeys operate via Lingfield

10 MAY 1950 Route 718 diverted between Walthamstow and Woodford Wells to run via Chingford

4 JULY 1951 New route 723A Grays-Aldgate via Belhus Park Estate

29 SEPT 1951 Route 727 last day of operation

30 SEPT 1951 Route 714 extended from Baker Street to Luton via 727

30 APL 1952 Route 723 diverted at Grays to run via Chadwell St. Mary and terminate at Tilbury Riverside Station.
Route 723A extended from Grays to Tilbury Civic Square via Dock Road

3 DEC 1952 Route 717 diverted between Woodham and Woking to serve Sheerwater Estate

6 MAY 1953 Route 723A diverted to terminate at Tilbury Riverside Station

2 JUNE 1953 Coronation Day—many routes split in London, several to finish at off-route terminals

1 JULY 1953 New route 725 Gravesend-Croydon-Kingston-Windsor

19 MAY 1954 Route 726 revised to operate from Romford-Whipsnade Zoo via Baker Street (Summer only)

7 JULY 1954 Route 723A curtailed at Grays
New route 723B Tilbury Riverside Stn.-Dock Road-Grays-Purfleet-Aldgate
New route 720A Aldgate-Harlow New Town-The Stow (via First Avenue)

5 OCT 1955 New route 716A Woking-Marble Arch-Stevenage
Route 717 revised to operate Victoria-Welwyn Garden City Stn. via Barnet, Welham Green and Hatfield

18 APL 1956 Route 717 diverted between Welham Green and Hatfield to serve South Hatfield

11 JULY 1956 Routes 712, 713 diverted between Borehamwood and Radlett to serve Theobald Street
Route 718 extended from Epping to Harlow New Town Centre via Brays Grove
New route 719 Hemel Hempstead-Victoria via Garston and Kingsbury
Route 720A extended to Harlow New Town Centre and diverted via Brays Grove

8 AUG 1956 New route 715A Hertford-Marble Arch via Hertford Heath and Edmonton

17 DEC 1956 'Suez Crisis'—fuel emergency situation leads to reductions over sections of the following routes—709, 712, 716, 718, 722, 725,

1 APL 1957 Fuel emergency ceases and full service restored

19 MAY 1957 Route 726 extended on Summer Sundays to Harold Hill

12 JUNE 1957 Route 717 extended in Welwyn Garden City to terminate at Cole Green Lane

28 JULY 1957 Route 721 certain journeys extended in Brentwood to terminate at Highwood Hospital on Sundays

16 OCT 1957 Route 709 journeys no longer double run to serve Amersham, The Crescent

8 JAN 1958 Route 722 diverted in Romford to serve Oldchurch Hospital

5 MAY 1958 The bus strike began and lasted until 20 JUNE 1958 during which time the following change was planned to take effect on 14 MAY 1958:
Route 707 certain journeys diverted to double run via Tatsfield

15 OCT 1958	Route 705 diverted to serve Hayes (Kent)
	Route 721 certain journeys extended in Brentwood to terminate at London Hospital Annex, daily
27 SEPT 1959	Eccleston Bridge completely closed for reconstruction—all coaches diverted via Elizabeth Bridge until 3 MAY 1961
11 SEPT 1960	Route 726 last day of operation between Romford and Harold Hill
23 NOV 1960	Route 712 diverted between Radlett and St. Albans to serve Park Street and Chiswell Green
	Route 716 diverted between Welwyn and Stanborough to serve Welwyn Garden City
	Route 717 diverted at Hatfield to serve Hollybush Lane and terminate at Welwyn Garden City Stn.
3 JULY 1962	Route 722 last day of operation of Hornchurch Station service
22 MAY 1963	Route 717 diverted via Welwyn Garden City to serve Queen Elizabeth Hospital
	Route 720 due to the opening of Harlow Garage when working journeys introduced from Bishop's Stortford to Harlow Bus Stn.
25 MAY 1963	New route 712A Dorking-Victoria-Park Street-Whipsnade Zoo to operate on Summer Sats. & Suns.
26 MAY 1963	Route 726 revised to operate Suns.-Fris. only (Summer only)
28 AUG 1963	Route 705 revised to operate 'Express' between Victoria and Windsor, with only 13 intermediate stops on this section, and diverted via Chiswick Flyover and Colnbrook By-Pass
18 NOV 1963	Route 722 extended from Corbets Tey to Dartford via Aveley and Dartford Tunnel
10 MAY 1964	Route 726 diverted between Golders Green and Friars Wash to run via Mill Hill and M1 Motorway
6 SEPT 1964	Route 712A last day of operation
3 NOV 1964	Route 703 last day of operation
4 NOV 1964	Route 709 revised on weekdays to operate 'Express' between Oxford Circus and Amersham and diverted between Shepherds Bush and Uxbridge to run via Western Avenue. Sunday service operates between Godstone-Baker Street Stn.
	Route 710 Sundays extended to Chesham to cover route 709
	Routes 712/713 service revised and new routes introduced:
	712B Dorking-Victoria-Park Street-Dunstable
	713A Victoria-Shenley-Luton (M-F peak hours only)
	Route 717 extended from Victoria to Wrotham via 703
	Route 722 withdrawn between Corbets Tey and Dartford
	Route 723 rerouted between Grays and Aveley to run via Belhus as route 723A
	Route 723A extended from Grays to Tilbury Riverside Stn. via Dock Road, no Sunday service
	Route 723B withdrawn between Tilbury and Grays
	Route 725 diverted to serve Ashford Town Centre
	New route 727 Express Tring-Victoria via Hemel Hempstead, M1 Motorway, Mill Hill, Golders Green running on Weekdays only
14 APL 1965	Routes 712/3 all suffix letters withdrawn—service pattern revised: Route 712 Dorking-Victoria-Park Street-Luton-Dunstable or Whipsnade
	Route 713 Dorking-Victoria-Shenley-St. Albans-Luton, Dunstable or Whipsnade
	Note: The Whipsnade service operates on Summer Sats. & Suns. only
MAY 1965	Route 727 diverted via Garston and Watford-By-Pass due to sudden closure of M1 motorway south of junction with M10
26 SEPT 1965	Victoria area one-way traffic scheme makes Eccleston Bridge one-way northbound. Southbound coaches stop in Buckingham Palace Road
3 OCT 1965	Route 707 extended from Oxted to Holland, Coldshott on Sundays
30 OCT 1965	Route 709 last day of Express operation
	Route 720A and 727 last day of operation
31 OCT 1965	Route 720 diverted to run via Harlow Bus Station to cover former route 720A
1 NOV 1965	Routes 701/2 split in London on Monday to Friday to operate Ascot or Sunningdale to Victoria and Hammersmith-Gravesend
	Route 709 curtailed to operate daily between Godstone-Baker Street Stn.
	Route 710 extended to Chesham daily to cover route 709
	Route 714 split at Baker Street Stn. on Monday to Friday to operate in two end-on sections
	Route 722 revised to operate on Monday to Friday peak hours only
10 JULY 1966	Route 706 extended on Summer Sats. & Suns. to Chartwell
	New route 724 Express one-man-operated, Romford-High Wycombe via Harlow, Hatfield, St. Albans, Watford and Amersham
30 DEC 1966	Route 723A last day of operation
31 DEC 1966	Route 709 revised to operate M-F peak hours and Sunday
	Route 710 withdrawn on Monday-Friday between Amersham-Chesham
	Route 711 diverted to run via Banstead Village
	Route 714 through Monday-Friday service reinstated
	Routes 714 and 718 diverted from Baker Street to serve Oxford Circus
	Route 715A revised to operate M-F peak hours and Saturdays
	Route 723B withdrawn between Aldgate and East Ham and revised to operate M-F peak hours and Saturdays
25 MAR 1967	Route 706 Summer extension to Chartwell now operates on Wed, Thurs, Sat & Sun
13 MAY 1967	New route 727 Express, one-man operated, Luton Stn.-Watford-Heathrow Airport-Kingston-Gatwick Airport-Crawley
12 AUG 1967	Route 702 withdrawn on Saturday between Sunningdale and Victoria
7 OCT 1967	Route 702 reinstated to Sunningdale on Saturdays
1 DEC 1967	Route 705 last day of express operation
2 DEC 1967	Route 705 revised to operate as route 704 between Victoria and Windsor
	Route 716A diverted between Little Heath and Lemsford, to cover route 717 withdrawal, via Welham Green, South Hatfield, Queen Elizabeth Hospital and Welwyn Garden City
	Route 717 curtailed to operate between Wrotham and Baker Street only
30 DEC 1967	Route 701 extended in Ascot to Heatherwood Hospital
15 APL 1968	Route 726 diverted via Oxford Circus
18 MAY 1968	Route 701 through M-F service reinstated
	Route 702 M-F service Victoria-Sunngingdale operates during peak hours only
8 JUNE 1968	Route 715A last day of Saturday operation
9 JUNE 1968	Route 707 last day of Sunday service between Chelsham and Holland (the remainder of the Sunday service from Aylesbury to Chelsham operates as route 706)
2 AUG 1968	Route 722 last day of operation
6 SEPT 1968	Route 726 last day of operation
4 OCT 1968	Route 723B last day of operation
22 NOV 1968	Route 717 last day of operation
23 NOV 1968	Routes 701, 702 converted to O.M.O.
	Route 710 converted to O.M.O. and revised to operate Amersham Garage-Baker Street Station via Marble Arch
	Route 711 converted to O.M.O. and diverted to double run to Gerrards Cross Packhorse
	Route 714 converted to O.M.O.
	Route 719 converted to O.M.O. and extended from Victoria to Wrotham to cover former route 717
	Route 720 converted to O.M.O.
14 FEB 1969	Route 707 last day of operation
	Route 715A last day of operation
15 FEB 1969	Route 706 converted to O.M.O. revised to operate Aylesbury-Chelsham, extended M-F peak hours to Westerham (double running to Tatsfield in direction of peak only). Summer Wed, Thur, Sat & Sun service to Chartwell continues to operate but not via Tatsfield
	Route 708 converted to O.M.O.
	Routes 712/713 converted to O.M.O. and Saturday service to Luton withdrawn, Whipsnade summer journeys now operate daily
	Route 725 converted to O.M.O.
1 JAN 1970	Under the Transport (London) Act, 1969 the Country Bus and Coach section of London Transport passed to a new company London Country Bus Services Ltd., a subsidiary of the

National Bus Company. In view of the changes since 1946 the complete Green Line network at this date is listed below:

701* Gravesend-Victoria-Ascot
702* M-F peaks Victoria-Sunningdale, Sats & Suns Gravesend-Victoria-Sunningdale
704 Tunbridge Wells-Victoria-Windsor
705 Sevenoaks-Westerham-Victoria-Windsor
706* Aylesbury-Victoria-Chelsham extended M-F peak hours to Westerham and summer Weds, Thurs, Sats & Suns to Chartwell
708* East Grinstead-Victoria-Hemel Hempstead
709 Godstone-Baker Street Stn. M-F peaks & Suns.
710* Amersham-Baker Street
711* Reigate-Oxford Circus-High Wycombe
712* Dorking-Victoria-Park Street-St. Albans-Dunstable
713* Dorking-Victoria-Shenley-St. Albans-Dunstable
Route 712/3 operate to Luton M-F peaks and to Whipsnade Zoo summer only
714* Dorking-Kingston-Oxford Circus-Barnet-Luton
715 Guildford-Oxford Circus-Enfield-Hertford
716 Chertsey-Marble Arch-Welwyn Garden City-Hitchin
716A Woking-Marble Arch-Welham Green-Welwyn Garden City-Stevenage
718 Windsor-Kingston-Victoria-Harlow
719* Wrotham-Victoria-Kingsbury-Hemel Hempstead
720* Bishop's Stortford-Harlow-Aldgate
721 Brentwood-Romford-Aldgate
723 Tilbury-Grays-Aveley-Aldgate
724* Express Romford-High Wycombe
725* Gravesend-Croydon-Kingston-Windsor
727* Express Luton Stn.-Heathrow Airport-Crawley
*one man operated

13 APL 1970 Routes 704, 705 diverted away from Eton due to closure of Windsor Bridge.

20 FEB 1971 Route 702 curtailed to operate Victoria-Sunningdale M-F peaks only, Sat & Sun service (Gravesend-Sunningdale) withdrawn
Route 710 curtailed to operate Amersham-Uxbridge Stn.
Routes 712/713 revised St. Albans-Dunstable section operates M-F peaks and Sundays, withdrawn between St. Albans and Luton
New route 723A Grays-Belhus Estate (Errif Drive)-Aldgate

20 MAR 1971 Route 727 Express extended from Luton Stn. to Luton Airport

15 MAY 1971 New route 715A Guildford-Kingston-Oxford Circus-Enfield-Hertford. Sats only

4 JULY 1971 Routes 704/705 extended from Windsor Bus Stn. to Windsor Safari Park on summer Sundays

1 JAN 1972 Route 721 converted to O.M.O.
Route 723 converted to O.M.O. with all journeys operating via Belhus Estate as former route 723A. Tilbury Terminal changed to Civic Square

5 FEB 1972 Route 718 converted to O.M.O.

11 MAR 1972 Routes 716/716A converted to O.M.O.

25 MAR 1972 Routes 704/705 converted to O.M.O.

29 APL 1972 Routes 715/715A converted to O.M.O.

3 JUNE 1972 Route 724 Express withdrawn between Rickmansworth and High Wycombe and diverted to run via Heathrow Airport to Staines

13 OCT 1972 Route 710 last day of operation

14 OCT 1972 Route 716 diverted in Stevenage to serve Lister Hospital Suns only

5 MAY 1973 Route 723 withdrawn between Tilbury and Grays

6 JULY 1973 Route 702 last day of operation

4 MAY 1974 Route 720 extended from Bishop's Stortford to Stansted Airport

31 MAY 1975 New route 703 Baker Street-Epsom-Dorking
Routes 712, 713 withdrawn between St. Albans and Dunstable and Victoria and Dorking
Route 712 revised to operate Victoria-Park Street-St. Albans weekdays only, extended summer to Whipsnade Zoo
Route 713 revised to operate Victoria-Shenley-St. Albans extended summer to Whipsnade Zoo
Routes 712, 713, 716, 716A diverted southbound via Baker Street and Oxford Circus

3 OCT 1975 Route 701 last day of operation

25 NOV 1975 Route 727 Express diverted to serve new Gatwick Airport terminal

14 MAY 1976 Route 716A last day of operation

15 MAY 1976 Route 709 converted to O.M.O.
Route 716 withdrawn from Chertsey and revised to operate Woking-Hitchin via former route 716A from Woking to Welwyn Garden City, Bridge Road thence via route 716 to Hitchin but serving Lister Hospital, Stevenage daily

3 SEPT 1976 Routes 712/713 last day of operation to Whipsnade Zoo

30 SEPT 1976 Route 706 last day of operation to Chartwell

1 OCT 1976 Route 703 last day of operation

28 JAN 1977 Routes 712/713 last day of operation

29 JAN 1977 New route 707 Victoria-Golders Green-Barnet-St. Albans-Luton Airport
New route 717 Express Victoria-Golders Green-Brent Cross Shopping Centre-Borehamwood-Shenley-St. Albans-Luton Airport
Route 714 revised to operate Dorking-Kingston-Victoria

26 MAR 1977 Route 715A last day of operation

1 APL 1977 Route 706 last day of operation
Route 720 last day of operation

2 APL 1971 New route 702 Bishop's Stortford-Harlow-Walthamstow Central Stn.
New route 703 Bishop's Stortford-Harlow-Epping-Waltham Cross (Weekdays only)
Route 708 extended from Hemel Hempstead Bus Stn. to Aylesbury to cover former Route 706
New route 710 Express Guildford-Ripley By-Pass-Kingston-By-Pass-Oxford Circus. MF peak hours only.
Route 715 rerouted daily to operate via Kingston over former 715A route
Route 718 curtailed to operate Windsor -Kingston-Victoria
Route 724 Express extended from Staines via Runnymede to Windsor Castle.

21 MAY 1977 New route 700 Express, summer only. Victoria-Windsor Bus Stn, calling only at Windsor Castle.
Route 704 diverted to double run via Heathrow Airport Central. Certain Sunday journeys diverted to operate via Knockholt Pound
Route 705 diverted to double run via Heathrow Airport Central. Certain journeys diverted to double run to Chartwell (except Mondays and Fridays)
New route 726 Gravesend-Windsor as existing route 725 but diverted at Ashford via Heathrow Airport thence non-stop to Windsor via M4

22 MAY 1977 New route 737 Express Victoria-Whipsnade Zoo via Golders Green, Mill Hill, M1 Motorway, Summer Sundays only

1 JULY 1977 Route 721 last day of operation

20 AUG 1977 Route 703 Sunday service introduced between Harlow and Waltham Cross

25 SEPT 1977 Routes 704, 705, last day of operation to Windsor Safari Park

30 SEPT 1977 Route 711 last day of operation

1 OCT 1977 New route 790 Victoria-High Wycombe-Amersham, joint service with Oxford route 290

19 NOV 1977 Route 708 certain journeys diverted to run via Brent Cross Shopping Centre on weekdays

14 JAN 1978 Route 716 curtailed to operate between Woking and Oxford Circus
New route 722 Hitchin-Welwyn Gdn City-Victoria
New route 732 Hitchin-Welwyn Gdn City-Brent Cross Shopping Centre-Victoria (weekdays only)

1 APRIL 1978 Route 708 curtailed to operate between Aylesbury and Victoria with certain weekday journeys running via Brent Cross Shopping Centre
Route 719 revised to operate between Hemel Hempstead and East Grinstead via Kingsbury, Victoria thence via former route 708
New route 729 Victoria-Borough Green M-F peak hours only, replacing route 719

16 APL 1978 New route 739 Victoria-Brands Hatch operating on major race days only

19 MAY 1978 Route 703 last day of operation—replaced by bus 329

20 MAY 1978 New route 701 Victoria-Windsor Bus Stn. extended daily during summer to Windsor Safari Park. This route runs non-stop via M4 motorway between Hammersmith and Heathrow Airport

21 MAY 1978 Route 705 revised to operate on Sundays only from Windsor Bus Stn to Tunbridge Wells via Westerham with certain journeys double running

	to Chartwell during the Summer. Rerouted away from Hayes (Kent) to serve Bromley Common Route 737 Express rerouted from Golders Green to run non-stop via M1
20 MAY 1978	New route 712 Bishop's Stortford-Harlow-Romford replacing sections of routes 703 and 724. No Sunday service Harlow-Bishop's Stortford Route 724 Express withdrawn between Harlow and Romford
28 OCT 1978	Route 725 rerouted to serve Bexleyheath
31 MAR 1979	Route 712 rerouted via Epping Forest, Wake Arms
2 APL 1979	New route 713 Bishop's Stortford-Harlow-Epping-Chigwell-Romford (Monday-Friday peak hours only)
28 APL 1979	Route 704 revised to operate between Windsor Bus Stn. and Victoria New route 706 Tunbridge Wells West Stn-Victoria via former route 704 Certain Sundays journeys operate via Knockholt Pound New Route 747 Jetlink non-stop Heathrow Airport-Gatwick Airport
29 APL 1979	Route 705 revised to operate Tunbridge Wells West Stn.-Westerham-Victoria on Sundays only. Certain Summer journeys double run to Chartwell
1 JULY 1979	Route 716 certain Sunday journeys revised to operate between Oxford Circus and Staines via Addlestone and Thorpe Park Leisure Centre
26 OCT 1979	Route 709 last day of operation
27 OCT 1979	Route 715 revised to operate between Guildford and Oxford Circus Route 719 revised to operate between Hemel Hempstead and Victoria via Kingsbury New route 734 Hertford-Wood Green-Brent Cross-Wembley-Hounslow-Heathrow-Staines-Thorpe Park-Addlestone New route 735 Hertford-Oxford Circus With the revision to routes 715 and 719 cross-London running which Green Line had started on 10 December 1930 ceased.

This page: Many strange vehicles have operated on Green Line including red STL2093 (A. B. Cross) and small Bristol BN30 (G. Brigden). Opposite page, top, left: RF70 at Heathrow Airport on the first day of Route 727 in May 1967. Top, right: RT4490 at Aldgate in 1962. Bottom, left: Airfix advertisement RP87 at Harlow. Bottom, right: Golden Jubilee livery is carried by RS137 as part of the 1980 celebrations (all B. J. Davis).